GREEN ARE MY MOUNTAINS

By the same author

Non-fiction
BLUE ABOVE THE CHIMNEYS
ROSES ROUND THE DOOR

Fiction
RHANNA
RHANNA AT WAR
CHILDREN OF RHANNA
RETURN TO RHANNA
SONG OF RHANNA
STORM OVER RHANNA

KING'S CROFT
KING'S ACRE
KING'S EXILE

GREEN ARE
MY MOUNTAINS

Christine Marion Fraser

COLLINS
8 Grafton Street, London W1
1990

William Collins Sons & Co. Ltd
London · Glasgow · Sydney ·Auckland
Toronto · Johannesburg

BRITISH LIBRARY CATALOGUING IN PUBLICATION DATA

Fraser, Christine Marion
Green are my mountains
I. Title
823′.914 [F]

ISBN 0-00-215445-5

First published 1990
Copyright © Christine Marion Fraser 1990
Set in Compugraphic Symposia by Burns & Smith, Derby
Printed and bound in Great Britain by
William Collins Sons & Co. Ltd, Glasgow.

For Mary Rachel,
as gentle as the green hills
and just as eternal

Contents

1

Draughts in the Attic

'Everything in this place leaks – even the dog!'

So quoth my daughter Evelyn, mournfully, and without so much as a twitch of her normally smiling lips. I just burst out laughing at the quaintness of the expression and before long we were both in a fine state of merriment. It was 1978, she was just eight years old and possessed of a happy-go-lucky nature that reminded me of my tomboy self when I was her age.

But what she said was apt enough. The roof of our cottage leaked like a sieve, and Tania, our big, lovable white Samoyed bitch, had been a martyr to a weak bladder ever since she had given birth to ten little Samoyed pups some six years previously. On a visit to the vet we also discovered that she suffered from a slight heart murmur, but in spite of her ailments she was a beautiful dog, sturdy and fun-loving, a true princess of her breed who smiled and posed for any camera and bared her teeth at Evelyn should she dare to try and oust her from the limelight.

Unlike Shona, our first adored Samoyed, Tania displayed a positive delight in dressing up. She would allow Evelyn to tog her out in bright red shorts, a frilly blouse and even a bonnet if she was in a good enough mood, and thus attired she grinned, romped about and never felt for one moment that we were laughing at her. She knew it was all a delicious joke in which everybody could share and enjoy to the full.

As for the roof, the surveyor's report had made light of it, possibly owing to the fact that there was no hatch into the roof space, and on the September day we moved in, it was to the discovery of soaked carpets and mattresses and the cold realization that there was no hot water in the house. This was another oversight by the surveyor who had spotted an immersion switch in a cupboard and had assumed it to be wired up.

But it wasn't, nor was there a hot water tank. In fact, there were no tanks of any description anywhere in the house. We had known that our water came straight from the hill, but in our ignorance we had imagined it to flow into some sort of holding tank in the house. It didn't. The plumbing was basic in the extreme, and if we hadn't been so exhausted that day of the flitting in a local plumber's van we might have done an about turn and flitted right back to our villa on the shores of the Holy Loch, with all the mod cons we had spent four years fitting in. But, of course, we didn't. Instead we had a jolly camp tea in the primitive kitchen and tumbled into our hastily made beds after humping the soaking mattresses outside. They had been left by the previous owner, and we didn't need them anyway, which was as well for us.

Next day, with the September sunshine streaming in through the windows, we forgot the leaks and the lack of hot water. This was our very own wee cottage. Bought and paid for from the proceeds of our other house. No mortgage, no debt. Ours! Ours! Ours! Right in the heart of a peaceful glen with no din from the Polaris base in the Holy Loch grinding into our lugs. Only the birds and the freedom and the wide blue yonder.

It was a glorious, wonderful feeling. Ken and I had often passed the cottage, and though it was a douce little place it was in a perfect setting and we had always thought how nice it would be to live there.

But it was with Mary, my darling half-sister, that I first saw inside the house. It had just come on the market, Mary was on holiday with us, and because Ken was working and unable to get away, it was she who came with me to get the keys.

From the very first moment I loved the house. Its tranquil atmosphere washed into my heart and remained there for all the hard but happy years we were to spend in it, and long after. The front door opened into a stone-floored porch, a step lower than road level. This probably owed itself to years of successive road resurfacing, but I gave no thought to the problems a sunken stone porch might bring. I was possessed with a mind that blithely skipped over life's impracticalities. I always saw just the things that appealed to me or what I wanted to see. What I saw then was a house with perfect access for a wheelchair – the front entrance, anyway. It didn't matter that the back of the house was higher than the front, or that the side door leading off from the porch gave out to several high steps all overgrown with grass and ferns.

What mattered was that I could get in from the front with very little bother. Our Holy Loch house had impossibly steep access from the road and that was one of our main reasons for wanting to leave it.

11

I simply charged through the rooms of the cottage, loving each one, knowing I had to have the place, thinking even that a big jawbox sink in a partitioned-off bit of the porch was all part and parcel of a real country cottage. A quick glimpse through a door at the back of the porch revealed a dingy, cramped bathroom with just a loo and a hideous iron bath.

It didn't matter! It didn't! I quickly convinced myself of this, even though I had always had a weakness for beautiful bathrooms and was particularly proud of the gleaming turquoise suite we had installed in the villa.

I think my longing for elegant porcelain stemmed from my Govan days when there was just a stairhead 'cludge' with newspaper squares pinned on the door and bigger squares decorating the scrubbed wooden floor. This had been a communal domain, and I will never forget my sojourns into its portals, sitting on the hard wooden pan with my knickers at my ankles while I followed the adventures of Oor Wullie and The Broons, squinting at the pages from the dim light filtering through the tiny frosted window with its covering of wire mesh and its broken pane covered over with a wooden panel.

This was my place of repose, the only way I could escape for a while our room and kitchen and my brothers and sisters warring with one another. Resentment burned in me if anyone dared to try the door whilst I was in residence, and, little devil that I was, I simply delighted in trying the patience of the Toilet Paper Lady, named so because she always came to the cludge armed with her own roll of toilet tissue and a look of positive disdain on her face for heathens who used newspaper squares, especially those torn from Labour-orientated publications.

In the years that followed I had always harboured a secret longing for a 'real' bathroom, and on moving to the Holy Loch I had gotten my wish. If we bought Polly Powdermill it would be back to square one in more ways than one, but I didn't want to think of that. Material things had never meant a great deal to either Ken or me. We had started out in married life with almost nothing and had very slowly and painfully built up our collection of household possessions. We both hated debt and had never been ones to rush out and buy things on the never never for the sake of making life easier, or to try and appear more affluent than we were.

When Evelyn was born I had thought the world was mine when Ken proudly bought me a brand new spin-dryer to make nappy-drying easier. I didn't own a washing machine then, and still didn't, and only recently had we purchased a second-hand fridge. We hadn't yet gotten over the novelty of making ice cubes, which we seldom used but kept them anyway, 'just in case'.

Since the age of ten, when I had fallen prey to a rare illness which ensured I would have to use a wheelchair for the rest of my life, I had managed to live without all the requisites that might have made my life easier. I was well used to just making do, and now I shut the door resolutely on the drab little bathroom and told myself that if we were lucky enough to get the cottage, we would get by as we had always done before.

What mattered most to me then was having a place where I could pursue my writing career in peace and tranquillity, and there was an abundance of that here.

Mary felt it too, and in her quiet, reassuring way advised me to try and make the house ours. 'It has a happy atmos-

phere, Chris, and both you and Ken will one day make it a
home to be proud of.'

When Ken saw it, he loved it too, and so we bought it,
knowing how much was needing to be done, but loving the
idea of living in the heart of a beautiful glen in a house
whose back windows gazed out on to the hills and the trees,
and where a river at the bottom of the field foamed into
deep cauldrons where salmon and trout lived in plenty. And
all around was the sky and the birds and the utter freedom
of the Highland countryside.

In those early days my euphoria knew no bounds.
Looming on the horizon was the publication of my first
novel *Rhanna*, and that was excitement enough to be going
on with. But now there was Powdermill Cottage, and I
simply revelled in the glowing autumn countryside and the
rapturous thought of living in that dear little house.

It was a drab, plain wee place when it came into our
hands. Happy the previous occupants might have been, but
they hadn't lavished much attention on their domain. The
exterior was supposed to be cream coloured, but had
weathered to a sickly grey-brown which was rapidly flaking
off the walls. The garden had once known tender, loving
care, but now it was an overgrown jungle of rampant rasp-
berry canes, bramble thorns, and tough moor grasses.

That, however, was the least of our problems. What
mattered to us was that a high wall, running from either end
of our cottage, enclosed acres of woodland and fields and
very effectively shut us off from the rest of the world. The
ruins of old buildings were dotted about everywhere, for
this had once been a thriving gunpowder mill that had
finally ground to a halt in the early years of this century.
Our cottage had been the under-manager's house and dated

back to the 1830s. The old changing sheds and the remains of the boilerhouse were situated in a leafy lane to the side of our house. Long ago, people from the village of Sandbank three miles away had trod up the Mill Brae every morning to the factory. Horses and carts bearing empty barrels from the cooperage at Sandbank had clip-clopped up the long, hard slope to deliver their load.

Ruins of the old stables at the foot of the lane were torn apart by tree roots, but they were still standing just the same. A little railway had once chanted its way through the mill; sluice gates on the river had controlled the flow of water; baffle walls, still almost as whole as the day they were erected, stood on the other side of the river, partially obliterated by thick undergrowth and trees but sturdily erect and providing a favourite shelter for the sheep who wandered the area.

At the foot of our garden, close to an overgrown ruin, we found a little gravestone dedicated to 'A faithful dog, Dash'. The date stretched back to the last century yet was perfectly readable and a solid testimony to someone who had loved and lost a beloved companion.

Perhaps he and his master had lived in our house. We all speculated, Evelyn with tears in her eyes for a little dog not forgotten but resting peacefully beneath the mossy earth, his gravestone a reminder that he had once lived and roamed these leafy glades.

It might sound creepy, to have all these ruined buildings round about us, but it wasn't. In all the years we lived there, even on moonlit nights with the owls hooting from the trees, we never felt spooky or afraid. Rather the past and the present mingled together in total harmony. We often went for walks through the mill, in daylight and gloaming and, of course, in moonlight.

*

Polly Powdermill was happy to have us living there. We could feel the quiet essence of contentment breathing out from the walls. It had been a neglected little house, but it knew all that was going to change and there was about it a secret air of anticipation for what was to come.

2

Polly Powdermill

Despite the fact that there were so many drawbacks to the cottage, we were extremely happy and busied ourselves settling in. Every morning Evelyn got the bus to her new primary school some four miles away, and Ken cycled to his job in the office of a local boatbuilders.

Left on my own I managed as best as I could in a house with very few facilities for an able bod, never mind someone in a wheelchair. Our water supply came straight off the hill by gravity feed from a five hundred gallon water tank situated a good way up the slope. That sounds like a lot of water but the inlet to the tank regularly silted up with pine needles and other sorts of debris, and if you didn't know what was happening you could find yourself suddenly without water, and, in my case, no way of getting to the tank to free the blocked pipe.

We were novices to this new way of life and had a long way to go before we got fly to the wiles of nature. Ken soon learned to leave me with a supply of brimming buckets, and on the days I was forced to use them I sweated and groaned as I filled pots to heat on our calor gas stove in order to wash dishes and clothes, and perform all the thousand and one water-dependent tasks about the house.

I had also quickly learned the inconvenience of a sunken porch. During heavy rain the water sluiced in under the front door until the place was swimming, and we were forced to lift the mouldy carpet placed there by the previous owners. Thereafter I simply opened the side door and brushed the water out, congratulating myself as I did so that the rain was saving me the effort of having to wash the porch in the regular way.

In between times I cleaned and cooked, and kept the living room fire going from the coal buckets which Ken had filled. Whenever I could, I set out blithely in my chair, with Tania at my side, to collect kindling for the fire.

How I loved that simple chore. The air smelt of apples due to a goodly supply of them growing in the confines of 'our estate' – as we gleefully liked to refer to the mill policies.

It was lovely wandering along the verges, watching lizards basking on sun-warmed rocks, identifying the numerous wild flowers, gathering twigs which were stuffed into a carrier bag hanging from the handle of my chair, feeling good and safe with my dog snuffling along at my side. I never felt lonely or afraid as long as she was beside me; a faithful, protective, big white shadow.

And the joy of going back to the little cottage among the hills, there to pile my twigs to dry in front of the fire, Jockey the Third, our new, young budgie, talking nineteen to the dozen in his cage by the window where he could watch the comings and goings of the wild birds.

He was a beautiful green budgie with a big, fluffy yellow head inside of which was the most intelligent brain I had yet encountered in the species. I delighted in him. He was the

18

most accomplished budgie I had ever known, quick to learn everything he could from the word go. He adored the human race and would rush to cling to the side of his cage to gaze enquiringly into any big human face that chanced along. It would have been too risky to allow him the freedom of our house – we fresh-air fanatics liked doors and windows to be opened whenever possible – but if I put my hand inside Jockey's cage, on to my finger he would quickly hop to listen to everything I had to say, his dear little yellow head cocked to one side as he devoured the words.

He wasn't just a mimic. If I started a sentence he would finish it and vice versa. From the day he learned to talk he devoted his life to public speaking, all in a broad Glasgow accent with the 'r's rolling off his tongue. He loved any word with an 'r' in it, and belted them out in a tough, very un-budgie sort of voice that was really comical to hear.

From the start he adored Tania. Whenever the furry white face appeared at his cage he went daft altogether, tweaking her nose and her long, pink tongue should she dare to allow it to dangle through the bars. She too had developed a special liking for the cheeky little guy. When visitors came she rushed to stand guard beside him with a look on her smiling Samoyed face that said, 'This bird with the human voice is mine, don't touch.'

Her amazement was a treat to behold when he first learned to say, 'Hello, Tania, give us a cuddle.' Up to his cage she would gallop to stare at him, her head on one side, a most anticipatory look on her doggie features as if she expected him to throw his wings round her at any moment and kiss her soundly on her wet black nose.

Happy first days, the sun streaming in through the windows, the tang of autumn sweet and heavy; the purple

19

hills, the buzzard soaring in the blue sky, the birds gradually coming to the bird table hastily erected by Ken and placed where we could see it, the drift of wood smoke hanging in the air. Evelyn loved her new school and soon made friends with children from a nearby farm whose house sat in the lee of a hill we could see from our rear windows.

Back in our tenement in the Govan days, our Mam, in the true style of the Aberdonian, had bestowed nicknames on everything and everybody, and I had picked this up from her. We weren't long at the cottage before I had christened people and places with my own personal tags. The green, rugged slope behind our house soon became Fraser's Hill, and no matter its geographical title it will always remain in my memory as our hill. The village was but a short walk from our cottage. Some folk called it Brig O'Doon, because if you blinked in the passing you might miss it. It seemed to belong to a past era in time. No unpleasing modern additions spoiled the appearance of the neat white cottages which had once housed the mill workers and their families. Sitting snug among the hills with the river meandering peacefully by, it was the most charming, unspoilt clachan I had yet seen. Once upon a time there had been a school, a church and an inn, but though the school was now a house, all trace of the others was long gone.

Over the road from us, in the grounds of what had once been the mill manager's house, there remained the ruin of a little shop. Some people remembered it as it had been, and Erchie, the fishman who came to our door once a week, told of the time when as a boy he came up the Mill Brae in a horse-drawn delivery van that carried stores for the shop, and for all the houses and farms scattered along the glen and beyond. The brae was so steep that only half the burden could be taken up the hill and unloaded. The horse and van had to go back down to collect the rest of the supplies which had been left at the Rumbling Bridge.

The people of the village were friendly, kind, and helpful. We loved them all from the start, especially snowy-haired Anne who still washed her pots and pans in the burn and had gone to the village school. She remembered the 'natural' hills of her childhood, grazed by sheep and cows, before armies of evergreens sprouted up. Many of the hills nearby were clothed in drab green, but those we could see from our windows were still the natural hills, dotted with real trees – oaks, birches and rowans, whose red berries made colourful splashes along the riverbank.

We congratulated ourselves for having been lucky enough to come and live in such a charming glen. So taken were we with the novelty we forgot what it was like to have hot water on tap and the luxury of a steaming hot bath. We all adapted quickly to alternative methods of keeping ourselves clean. We steeped and sponged quite cheerily in front of the fire, though if Evelyn had had her way she could happily have done without washing at all.

She was like a boy, with ragged knees and holes in the seat of her pants, and more often than not she came in from play covered in mud and grime. But she was as happy as a sandboy, always with a cheerful smile on her dirty little face. When the time came to peel off her trousers for bed, they could almost stand up by themselves, and I was faced with the never-ending task of keeping both Evelyn and her clothes as clean as possible without either a washing machine or a regular supply of hot water.

Meanwhile, the roof still leaked and went on leaking,

even though we paid a man sixty pounds to fix it. He did his best, but in his opinion we needed a new roof and since that was as impossible as a holiday on the moon we just smiled politely and prayed for a dry winter. Soon after that, Ken cut a hole in the ceiling of the room that was storing all our goods and chattels till we were dry enough to sort them out into drawers and wardrobes.

Every bucket and bowl in the house was transferred to the loft and after that it was a case of juggling them about, according to wind direction.

I can well remember lying in bed, listening to the drumming of rain on the roof and hoping that the drips were being caught. We became experts at knowing if this was the case or not. A dry, brittle sound told us that the rain was bouncing directly on to the beams, and with a few curses and groans Ken would have to rise from his warm bed to climb into a spidery loft to rearrange the buckets and bowls. If it was a deep, plummy plop, everything was all right and we would turn over and go to sleep with easy minds.

It was I, when I was quite alone in the house, who discovered that as well as owning a leaky roof, we also owned a cracked WC. People say that the events of your life pass before your eyes when you are drowning. During the split moment of my discovery that the WC was cracked, it wasn't my life that flashed before my eyes, it was certain items of my apparel that I had always believed could only achieve such contortions hanging from one peg on a windy washing line.

There I was one minute, sitting on the loo, quite at peace

with the world, and the next minute a tortuous crack split my eardrums. Before I knew what was happening I was catapulted to the floor together with a tide of water and a huge chunk of vitreous enamel bearing the proud logo of Shanks of Barrhead. Only I was too shocked at the time to know what it said or even to begin to think what had happened. All I could see were my knickers and my tights waving high in the air while the other half of me wallowed among water and broken porcelain.

I have never been one to cry out or make any sort of fuss during moments of dire distress, and I didn't let the side down now. But Tania had heard the noises, and from the living room she came galloping along to push open the loo door, there to stand and stare in comical amazement at her normally self-contained mistress.

I just lay where I was, covered in slosh and wet knickers, and laughed my head off, and with a certain amount of relief Tania barked and laughed too and romped in with wagging tail to embrace me with smiles and licks. She obviously thought I had staged the whole thing for her benefit.

The very next day the broken WC was replaced with a new one, and soon after that Ken removed the bath since all it was doing was taking up precious space. Round the side of the house it was carted and deposited beside the remains of a ruined building attached to the west gable of our house. We had been told that it had once been part of the under-manager's office, but all that was left now was a south-facing wall all of three feet thick, with window and door apertures gazing blankly out to the hills. I was enjoying demolishing it brick by brick when the rest of the family were at work and school.

'At least we'll have plenty of stones to build rockeries,'

Ken said optimistically. 'Hundreds of them.'

'Rockeries,' I said dreamily, seeing in my mind's eye trails and trails of colourful blooms everywhere. Forcing my mind back to the reality of a jungle-like 'garden' with no sign of cultivation anywhere, I looked fondly at the bath which hitherto I had hated. 'This could be a start,' I planned eagerly. 'We could build stones around it and fill it with earth and plant millions of flowers.'

'It would be great for tadpoles,' Evelyn said thoughtfully, not hearing a word I had said. 'We could get dozens of them in there and put in big stones for them to sit on when they turn into frogs.'

'We'll see, when the time comes,' I told her, knowing full well that the time of the tadpoles would come first, since a thousand and one practicalities would take precedence over fanciful notions of rockeries and flowers.

Mum Cameron, whom we now just referred to as Gran since Evelyn's birth, duly came to visit us from her top villa flat on the shores of the Holy Loch. Her reaction was one of horror when she saw the swimming porch, the draughty little cludge, and me on my knees at the fire trying to light it with damp twigs. Her jaw visibly fell open on its hinges when a cheeky mouse darted past her vision on its exit from the kitchen via the waste pipe under the sink.

'Are you sure you've done the right thing?' she squeaked, eyeing my grimy white face with some dismay.

She had good reason to ask such a question, because in the difficult days we ourselves sometimes wondered if we had made a good move, and I suppose the strain of coping with such inadequate facilities must have showed on our faces. But the next time she came a cheery fire was leaping up the lum and the little house looked most welcoming bathed as it was in sunshine. Tania was cosily ensconced on the hearthrug, in a tough gruff Glasgow voice Jockey was ordering Ken to make the dinner, then adding in a thoughtful mutter, 'Granny's a dinner.'

He often got his sentences mixed up like this and the results could be hilarious. (My ready imagination immediately provided me with a vision of Granny simmering merrily in a giant pot on top of the stove then being transferred to an enormous plate, there to lie gently steaming away.)

Not that she would have been a source of good eating, as she herself would have been first to admit. At school she had been known as 'the galloping hairpin' and to this day she was thin and wiry with a marked tendency to scuttle about hurriedly.

'Did I hear him saying my name?' she enquired, cocking a lug in Jockey's direction.

She always could take any amount of fun poked at herself, and on being told what the budgie had said she giggled and tucked into her tea.

'You've made a good move,' she decided firmly. 'This house has got potential and knowing you two you'll make it a place to be proud of.'

When she was taken for a most enjoyable ramble through the mill to pick apples and brambles for jelly making, her convictions were further strengthened and Ken and I smiled at one another over her head. Of course we had made a good move. Any doubts we had harboured were gradually dispersing and none of us had hankerings for the house by the Holy Loch.

This was our own little cottage, fully detached and self-contained, the first house we had ever lived in that wasn't connected to someone else's property. In a burst of affection I called the house Polly Powdermill. It would never go on the gate but would always be my own name for it and I sat down and wrote the following poem:

The old house,
in the lee of the hill,
Surrounded by relics
of the old powder mill.

The ancient stones silent,
the water wheels still,
But yet there is life
in the ruins of the mill.

The birds and the sheep
find shelter to sleep.
The fishermen fish
in the river so deep.

The flowers of the forest
carpet the glades.
And the frogs they are leaping
down in the lades.

Laughter bygone
forever is still
Yet the echoes still linger
here in the mill.

Voices come whispering
from the century that was
And Dash is just resting
under the moss.

On nights of bright moon
flooding over the hill
I sense the life breathing
here, in the mill.

And here in the house
time beats gently past
As it has done before
and will to the last.

3

Compliments of the House

The launch of my first novel, which was all about the lives, loves and passions of the characters of an imaginary Hebridean island called Rhanna, was no longer looming on a far horizon. The time for it was almost here and if I dared allow myself to think about it too much I felt sick with apprehension.

Letters came from my publishers, Blond & Briggs, outlining plans for the launching. We had no phone in the house, and after years of subservience to the beast, we had no desire to have one, so Ken walked up to the village phone box which was to be his 'country office' for many years to come. He made calls to various people connected with publishing and didn't tell me I was to appear on television and be interviewed on radio and by newspaper reporters. It was as well that he held his counsel. Just the excitement of knowing I was going to Glasgow to launch my first book was almost too much for me to bear, and the nearer the day came the less I was able to sleep at nights.

I had only a vague idea of what was entailed. If someone had told me I was to sit on a platform and make a champagne toast to a pile of hardbacks, I might have believed that a small grain of truth was lurking somewhere. But only a small grain. I was a Govan lass after all, and not so easily taken in.

Right from the start I had had no option but to put on a brave face and take all the knocks that life in a Glasgow tenement had to offer. But I had known what to expect from that kind of life. The world of publishing was another matter entirely. It was new and almost unbearably exciting for me – and Ken, too, for that matter. We anticipated the trip to Glasgow with a mixture of awe, wonder, and nail-biting trepidation.

The great day dawned at last, 15 November 1978. Jockey, Tania and Evelyn were safely deposited with Gran in her Holy Loch house, though it was with great reluctance that Evelyn abandoned the idea of coming with us.

'I would have stayed as quiet as a mouse,' she informed us sulkily, but Ken told her firmly that she had school to think of and so she stumped up Gran's stairs, carrying her suitcase and wearing a most belligerent scowl on her face. But at the last moment she relented, and down she flew to kiss us both soundly and wish us luck while into my hand she slipped a grubby piece of paper. It proved to be a drawing of her famous birds. Marvellous creations they were, of grinning bird caricatures with big clumpy feet and knobbly knees. She had always endowed them with the most amazing abilities. They could climb up perpendicular walls and hang stolidly from ceilings and rooftops with perfect ease. Over acres of paper the big feet clumped and hung, and in the drawing she handed to me there they were, climbing and clinging to gaily coloured books. One bird had nonchal-

29

antly entwined its lumpy knees round the big 'G' of a good luck message. Issuing from its mouth was a huge bubble which proudly proclaimed: 'My Mum's gonna be famous. Good luck, Christine Marion Fraser. From Tania, Jockey, Evelyn and me.'

I laughed with the sheer joy of those birds. They were so uninhibited, so daring and free. If I asked her to draw one now, she wouldn't be able to, and I'm sorry that I didn't keep them. I could have looked back and remembered in detail one small girl's view of the world around her.

We kissed and hugged all over again and then it was back to a strangely empty house where even the very mice seemed to be in hiding. There were none to greet us when we switched on the lights.

That night I didn't sleep well, but as usual Ken had to be bullied awake. To this day I honestly believe that the world could tumble about his ears and he would wake up in heaven and herald in the New Dawn with a series of unintelligible groans and grunts. After a few moments of this his mouth would begin to form sounds that were comprehensible to the human ear, at least to my human ear. I doubt if the uninitiated could make much sense of, 'Aah! Grump! Mmm! Ooh! Whasa time?'

When I had taken as much of this as I could, I lost my patience and hurled a few snarled orders at him, since morning does not bring out the sweetness in my nature and my fellowman had better watch out – or else!

Then came the next procedure of the day, the placing of a cup of tea into my bleary-eyed husband's outstretched paw, followed by a short lecture on how lucky he was to be wakened with a piping hot cuppy, one of the few men in the land, no doubt, to enjoy such a privilege. The tea came from the Teasmade on my side of the bed, one of the few luxuries we had brought with us from our last house, and one which I blessed every morning of my life. Revived by the beverage, Ken moved on to the next item on the agenda, this being a slurred and disgruntled rendering of his own particular version of the weather forecast.

'Huh! I see it's bloody raining again!' was the normal report. Other mornings could be more favourable, 'Don't tell me the sun's shining. Mmm, it's never a good sign if it starts off too bright. It'll likely rain by the time we get up.'

On this particular morning he fired off as usual, 'Are these grey clouds I see up there? God! Just like the thing. The place will likely be flooded by the time we get home again...'

I got out of bed. 'Come on, get up,' I ordered impatiently. 'This is the day! The day *Rhanna* gets launched. There will never be another day like it.' The full import of my words drove the last remnants of sleep out of his head, and five minutes later he was up and scurrying, a bit like the way Gran scurried when she was rushed and excited.

We had splashed out on some new clothes from my mail order catalogue, which was about the only way we could afford to buy clothes then, but before Ken could change into his he had to make a last-minute check of the attic. I heard him scraping about, playing draughts with the buckets, cursing a bit as his feet sent one clattering on the rafters. Some minutes later he clambered down, scraping cobwebs out of his hair, beating dust from his jersey, then it was a rush to get ready and he scooted away to the kitchen jawbox for a quick wash.

When we were both finally attired in our glad rags we spent another five minutes bolstering up one another with compliments. I had been blessed with a head of thick, naturally curly hair and could count on two fingers the number of times I had visited a hairdresser. For this occasion, however, I had had my curls tamed and trimmed. Ken looked very handsome in his good suit, his beard and moustache clipped to rather startling neatness, his hair cut to an obedient length by my own fair hands. I had always kept his red-gold locks tidy and he had always been satisfied with my efforts. He saw no reason to 'waste good money' even for the launch of *Rhanna*.

There was a moment of silence while we cocked our ears upwards. The plip-plops were good and plummy. As long as there were no cloudbursts in our absence the buckets wouldn't overflow. We could only hope for the best and we rushed away in our little blue Mini, leaving behind our mice and our sloping floors, our swimming porch and our leaky roof, exchanging it all for a brief two days in the comparative opulence of the Albany Hotel in Glasgow.

There we were met by Bob Cowan, Hutchinsons' (the publishers) representative for Scotland, but who, over the years, had become much more than that. He was a talent seeker in the literary world and had a nose for sniffing out a good book. He had also been launching authors for a good number of years and had been commissioned by Blond & Briggs to look after me. Bob was not a man of tall stature, but to me he seemed six feet tall as, with the utmost aplomb, he marched me in and out of the most nerve-racking situations.

No sooner had the electrically-operated doors of the Albany glided open (wonderful invention! 'Had they been installed specially for me?' I managed to joke, despite my jellified tum) than I was met by Max Hodes of the *Daily*

Record. Quaking, shivering, trembling in my wheels, I somehow managed to look and sound like a rational human being who was used to such attentions and was even enjoying them. But Max Hodes was a pretty easy guy to talk to, and he put me so much at ease that I was more than ready for the next reporter – and the next. The vanity that is inside every human being blossomed inside of me with such profusion that I suffered an attack of verbal diarrhoea, and the shorthand notes of one reporter went flying off the page.

After the reporters came lunch with the well-known Scottish writer, Jack House, whom my mother had spoken of with great fondness when I was a child. He told me he hadn't expected me to be so young, which made me think that most people harbour a notion that writers must be quite old in order to have stored up enough wisdom to enable them to write books. Later on this theory proved to be true enough, as I was to find out from face-to-face encounters with readers who expressed the same sentiments as Jack House. But I loved him for saying what he did, as, by the time I met him, I was feeling jaded and at least a hundred years old, and I had only been in Glasgow a mere two hours!

In the afternoon, a live radio interview at the BBC recording studios just about ripped apart my already frayed nerves. There I was, enclosed in a glass box, outside of which was Bob Cowan and Ken and all sorts of technicians. Large earphones were clamped to my red-hot lugs and my bulging eyes surveyed with horror a large radio microphone into which I had been instructed to speak to a disembodied lady interviewer in the Edinburgh BBC studios. Cheerful, robust and seemingly brimming over with interest about

Rhanna, she plied me with questions for which I had no ready answers. What had prompted me to write about an imaginary Hebridean island? From where had I got the idea? Could I give the listeners a hint, just a teeny little hint, of which island in the Hebridean group I had based my island upon?

How could I give her the answers to things I didn't know myself? Rhanna had just happened. There had been no prompting from any source except that which was inside of me, and when I had started writing about my island I had never even visited the Hebrides, let alone based my book on any particular one. Perhaps I had lived there in a past life, perhaps there existed such a phenomenon as inherited memory, I didn't know. All I knew was that Rhanna and the people who lived on it were as real and familiar to me as the face that looked back at me every morning from the mirror. And of course there was always my own extraordinarily active imagination to take into account and – I didn't want to appear to be big-headed – the gift for writing that had been born in me, and which just grew and grew with the passing years, whether I liked it or not.

What is your secret? The lady interviewer didn't in fact ask me that one, but it is a question I have often been asked since. I don't think it is a secret, it's just something that is mine, but if it is a secret then it grew with me in the womb where all of life's mysteries begin for every one of us.

The voice in my ear was rhyming off names. Skye? Rhum? Mull? Eigg? (Earlier on, Jack House had been of the opinion that my island must surely be based on Eigg and I had given him a cold look.)

'No, no, definitely not Eigg!' I babbled into the microphone.

'Where, tell me where?' almost sang the lady with the utmost gaiety, but did I detect a trace, just a weeny thread, of impatience?

'Inside my head, that's where, it grew inside my head!' I cried in confused desperation.

'I see, oh well, Christine, if you *must* keep us guessing then it's no use twisting your arm...'

I was very glad that a goodly number of miles separated us. There were more than radio waves coming over the air and I was very glad to take off the earphones and escape into the sane madness of the Glasgow streets, through which Bob drove us with happy ease. He was beginning to relax a bit. Only two TV interviews, he told me blithely, and it was nearly over for that day.

'Only two!' I yelped. 'Oh, God! Oh, help!' I groaned.

Ken squeezed my hand. 'You can do it,' he whispered. 'I'm proud of you, lamb, truly proud.'

His hand was warm and firm. What a comfort. What a helpmate. Always there, encouraging, supporting, guiding.

And I did do it. One interview in a lounge of the hotel, another in the STV studio at Cowcaddens. I sweated under blinding lights and spoke into great furry marrows, once I had ascertained they were microphones and not huge fluffy dusters coming to give me a quick mop-up. In both instances, while I wasn't exactly star quality, I knew I hadn't done too badly. There had been real flesh and blood interviewers, eyeball-to-eyeball sort of stuff. Nothing could be half so terrible as the radio interview, the awful sound-proof glass tank and a voice that might have come from Mars, so detached and distant had it been.

After that, Bob was so relieved and relaxed he just

seemed to melt into one big, happy smile. Back at the hotel he had a drink with us before disappearing homewards, and then it was just Ken and me, eating dinner in a softly lit room, being waited on hand and foot, and forgetting all the worries of the day in a haze of absolute wellbeing.

We were exhausted by the time the lift whizzed us up to our room, but bed was not uppermost in our minds. Can you guess what we both wanted more than anything? More than sleep, more even than a long-awaited cup of tea?

A bath! Just that. Oh glorious, tantalizing thought. A dream, just minutes away and no sniffly, pink-nosed little mice to witness proceedings. Being the star of the day I was graciously permitted to go first. Bliss! I wallowed, I steamed, I steeped, and made bubbles with the sponge until a huge yawning hint outside the door reminded me that this perfumed luxury was of limited duration.

When at last we were tucked up in bed we reviewed the events of the day. Soon I would be news. People would be reading glowing accounts (I had no knowledge then of ruthless book critics) of me and my literary efforts and a bit about our lives in a remote country cottage which we had painted as every author's dream. We hadn't mentioned the mice or the leaks or the lack of piped hot water. It is the natural instinct of many human creatures to pretend to the world that things in their life are better than they really are. No one likes to be thought of as poor, and of course there's the question of pride. Above all, there is the fear of the world getting to know more than is good for your image, especially if your name might one day be known beyond the boundaries of Dunoon, Scotland.

Anyway, we lay in bed sniffing one another appreciatively. We talked and recalled the absolute thrill of lying back earlier on the self-same bed watching me being interviewed on BBC television.

Of course I had worn all the wrong clothes! My hair wasn't right! I shouldn't have worn so much eye shadow. And did I really smile in that crooked fashion and sound like a Glasgow fishwife on a bad day?

And after torrents of self-criticism, I had lain back and wallowed in Ken's reassuring praise and admiration and his convincing reiterations that I was a natural born film star.

'Well, maybe not exactly a film star,' he amended, laughing. 'Certainly natural born.'

He was so happy to see all my dreams coming true at last, my hard work paying off, and we were both ready to laugh at anything that night with all the tensions and excitement behind us. Beyond the window, the lights of Glasgow lit up the sky, the traffic droned. Our little cottage in the glen seemed a million miles away. Quiet, dark and rainwashed hills belonged to another world.

'It's been great,' Ken murmured sleepily, 'but it will be nice to get home.' Home! Sweet word. Home in the faraway hills, with the gloaming silent all around, yet filled with the natural sounds of the country.

'Ay, home,' I sighed and breathed deeply the remains of bathtime aromas that owed themselves to neat little sachets and packets that had come with the compliments of the Albany Hotel.

And home we did go, after one more day of less hectic publicity, and one more night of scented bath luxury. Into my bag I placed everything bearing the logo 'With the compliments of the Albany Hotel'.

'You can't take these, Chris!' remonstrated a shocked Ken, as I calmly popped a sachet of bath foam into my case.

'Compliments of the house,' I laughed, following the foam with a dainty bar of wrapped soap. 'Everybody does it, some people even take the towels.'

'You're not! You're an author! Authors don't take things like towels from hotel bedrooms.'

'Oh, no, not the towels,' I returned reprovingly, 'that would be stealing.'

'But, the bath foam! We don't have a bath!'

'We will, someday we will,' I told him, optimistically and stubbornly.

He stood looking at me, his moustache bristling a bit, then with a snigger he snatched up a plastic bath cap and stuffed it into the side of his case. I knew he would suffer a mild form of mental torture until we were safely in our car. The suitcase might burst open in the foyer and there, revealed, would be the little shower cap, lying exposed for all the world to see. It didn't matter that the packet containing it told us it was a present from the hotel. He had taken it, and that was that, and I had to hide a smile when I noticed him securing one of his trouser belts round the case because 'the catch isn't too good'.

But he wasn't nearly as conventional as he had been when first we met. In those days he had been strictly obedient to rules and regulations, dos and don'ts. He had changed a lot over the years and told me it was my influence. Good or bad? Nobody should be ramrod straight. In the end they are the ones liable to snap. 'A happy medium.' Mam had always maintained that. She was right!

*

Down in the foyer all was quiet, with businessmen meandering through their staid lunches in the partitioned sitting areas. Bob Cowan, the reporters, the TV crews had departed. Normality had returned to our lives and we experienced a sense of deflation.

As we were going towards our little Mini, the most inconspicuous vehicle in the hotel car park, a group of office workers passed by.

'Oh! There's that lassie who was on telly the other night!' exclaimed one young woman in an awed sort of voice.

I glowed inside and looked at Ken. He was smiling and proud-looking. We both knew that our lives would never be normal again – and that this was just the beginning.

4

Winter Visitors

The winter moved on and the mice moved in – with a vengeance. We heard them scampering in the loft, we saw them diving into various gaps in the skirting whenever a light was snapped on in the kitchen. They had a merry time with our stored possessions in the Nothing Room, a small, dismal, unused box room leading off from the kitchen, and feasted on anything they could get their teeth into.

It was ridiculously easy for them to gain access into the house. The cold water pipe to the sink came up through a hole in the floor from a crude little basement which had a low door leading in from the back of the house. The mice made cosy winter nests in this rubble-strewn space, and when they were hungry they simply popped aloft, using the pipe to gain entry into the sink cupboard. They gnawed carpets, lino, wood, food and soap. It became the rule rather than the exception to find a bar of green Fairy kitchen soap pitted and scarred with toothmarks.

As fast as Ken filled the holes they reopened them. The entire kitchen would have to be gutted and sealed and possibly refloored, and because we were so busy with other things as well as keeping ourselves windproof and water-tight, such a big undertaking would have to wait for warmer weather, not to mention the money for materials. The second half of my advance for *Rhanna* had been due on publication but that had been weeks ago and there was still no sign of it and it would be many months before I was due any royalties on the book. Advances were not presents from publishers to authors. They were set against any royalties that might accrue at a later date, and were deducted from any payments due. So we had to get by as best we could, hope for better and richer days ahead, and in the meantime share our home with a host of furry lodgers. When Ken's brother John and his wife Doreen came to visit us from Glasgow, we hardly touched on the inconveniences, rather we waxed lyrical about our darling Polly Powdermill and they in turn went into raptures over the cottage and the surrounding countryside. The big attraction for many urban-based visitors was our real 'live' roaring log fire, which was certainly a welcoming sight in its Fyfestone setting.

The charms of the cottage were many and varied, so much so that people tended to overlook the lack of amenities, and because we made light of them a lot of our visitors weren't even aware that we lived without the kind of things they took for granted. Certainly Doreen and John were not in the least put out when they had to pay a visit to our bare little cludge, and anyway, what did it matter when everything else was so attractive?

I remember all of us talking nineteen to the dozen when, from the corner of my eye, I became aware of a tiny furry shape slinking along by the living room skirting. Horror and delight struggled in my heart, as this time it wasn't a mouse but a dear little shrew, its long hairy snout poking and snuffling into the carpet pile – although there wasn't much pile to snuffle into. Our new and beautiful carpets had been sold with the Holy Loch house and those we had inherited with the cottage were dingy and somewhat threadbare. Thrilled though I was to observe the little animal, which was a pygmy shrew known in Scotland as the 'wee thraw', I was not unaware of its mean and vicious nature which could motivate it into sinking its orange-red tipped teeth into anything that provoked it.

So it was with tightly held breath that I watched its progress, all the while praying that Doreen wouldn't see it and maybe start screaming, or that Tania wouldn't see it and maybe start a shrew hunt.

The wildlife both in and out of the house was to her a highly exciting form of entertainment, though it was doubtful if she would know what to do with a mouse even supposing one chanced into her smiling jaws. She would lie for hours anywhere in the house, her nose pressed firmly against a bolt hole, her cocked ears listening to rustlings and scrapings, her tail twitching while every so often she issued grunts and snorts of anticipation according to the strength of mouse odour. 'Mouse' was all we needed to say to send her dancing into the kitchen to check up on the activities of Mickey, Minnie, or both.

In this instance, however, she was too taken up with the visitors to pay heed to much else, and it was Evelyn who took the matter out of my hands.

'Aw, look,' she breathed lovingly, 'a wee shrew, oh, I wish I could catch it and keep it.'

'A wee what?'

Doreen was up on her two feet, Tania was up on her four. The tiny animal sensed danger. The kitchen with its many escape routes was a long way off, and chattering in alarm it darted across the floor. With a snort of pleasure Tania darted after it, while Doreen glanced wildly about and looked as if she would like to be darting too – straight out of the door!

All over the living room floor scooted the minuscule shrew, with Tania hot on its heels, and all we could do was watch the small drama in complete fascination.

The little animal led Tania a merry dance. It scampered under chairs, bobbed in and out of the furniture; climbed one and a half curtain lengths; dropped back to the floor to hide under a bookcase for a full minute before showing its furiously twitching nose once more. Rearing up on its hind legs it emitted a piercing shriek which was surprisingly loud coming from such a tiny throat.

'Will it attack?' wondered Doreen in a small voice, just as the shrew took off once more, playing 'Ring a Roses' round one of the dog's back legs, much to Tania's complete amazement. If she had had time to think about it, all she needed to do was to sit down and flatten the shrew and that would have been the end of the matter. But too late, the chase was on once more, until, beside herself with frustration, she sat back on her haunches as if not quite knowing what her next move should be.

With a sigh of exhaustion she flopped on the floor to stare at the tiny creature. It stared back cheekily, and then, quite suddenly, with a flick of its long tail and a last, defiant scream, it popped into a crack under the stone hearth and was never seen again – at least, not in the vicinity of the living room.

'Do they often come in like that?' Doreen asked faintly.

Evelyn opened her mouth, Ken got there first. 'Och, just

once in a while,' he said nonchalantly. Evelyn's mouth shut with a snap. She knew it would be better for her to keep it that way.

In truth, Ken was feeling pretty restricted at this time. The house was impossible for me to manage the way it was, and he had left his job in order to look after things. Not that he shed much tears leaving a place that had heaped too many responsibilities on his shoulders for too little reward. Being a professional artist he knew he would get enough freelance work to keep the wolf from the door, and I was certainly relieved to have him at home. I simply could not keep going with my writing and manage the house in its present state. So he applied for and received a pittance from the DHSS and with that we had to keep going, although there was little or nothing left over from household expenses to buy the material we so sorely needed for the cottage.

Ken filled mouseholes, he juggled the buckets about in the loft, he cut wood for the fire, and kept the water running when it looked like silting up or freezing up or both. By dint of much hard work he reorganized the house and got us all settled into our respective rooms. Somehow we managed to keep cosy despite the draughts that whistled under doors and through windows.

There were only two fireplaces in the house, one in Evelyn's room which had once been a parlour, and one in the living room where there had once been a kitchen range. Because there were no cupboards in the house, we still had to keep much of our bits and pieces in the Nothing Room. A cavity in the living room, once containing a hole-in-the-wall bed, had been boarded over with panel plank. But we were unaware of that then, nor did we know that a cupboard in Evelyn's room had also been boarded over.

Wood panelling had been used extensively throughout the house in an effort to cover the many flaws, and no doubt it had been quicker to board up the bed cavity and the cupboard rather than to do something useful with them. These were discoveries for the future. Meantime, Evelyn, an avid reader of Enid Blyton's Famous Five, thrilled to the idea that some secret cupboard might exist in her room.

Over the walls we would go, tap tapping, I willingly entering into the spirit of the thing for I had never quite gotten over the Famous Five myself. I still delved into boarding school yarns and was able to discuss with my daughter the escapades and adventures which kept her entranced for hours. Much later on in my writing career a family friend said to me, 'You must of course have read the classics,' and when I replied, 'Oh, yes, *What Katy Did, The Chalet School* stories and a host of others,' his face was a picture I shall never forget.

The wall-tapping was all part of the game, Evelyn fairly holding her breath as she knocked and listened and spoke of enchanted doors that opened into fabulous lands.

Our hidden cavities might only have been very mundane affairs, with no magic fairylands on the other side, but they would have provided us with much needed space. But, as a wardrobe had been placed in front of one and a bookcase in front of the other, many moons would pass before our questing fingers discovered those precious hollows. We had good fun just the same, tapping and listening and – in Evelyn's case – hoping never to find the thing she pretended most to desire. One never knew, it might house a dead body, or – horrors! her eyes big and round – the proverbial skeleton, all rattly bones and parched yellow skin and a jaw that flew open to reveal a big, toothy, mocking grin.

That first winter our visitors were many and varied. Everyone, it seemed, wanted to see for themselves what had lured us away from our comfortable flat to a remote cottage in a lonely glen. In a steady stream they came, often at the most unsuitable times, but come they did, morning, noon, and night. The tag 'writer' was attached to me now, and it was in the nature of people to want to know just what kind of abode a real live author must live in.

Both Ken and I had appeared in the newspapers, I had been heard on radio, seen on TV. Most were charmed by the house, the mice behaved well and kept out of the way, we joked about the roof and dwelt long and loudly on the delights of living deep in the country. No one ever seemed to want to 'pay a visit', so we were able to keep our poky little cludge a dark, family secret.

Always there was the novelty of a 'real' fire; soft lamplight gave the panel plank walls an olde worlde appearance; the views from the windows were much appreciated; our descriptions of country pursuits drew forth murmurs of envy. Tea, cake and gossip were dispensed and devoured, and both Ken and I sometimes wondered how long we could go on affording our 'sightseers'.

The second half of my advance for *Rhanna* had still not materialized, and with Christmas approaching we were getting both worried and despondent. To make matters worse, a most unwelcome visitor arrived in the form of a DHSS inspector. He had seen all my publicity stuff and had thought it time to have a sniff into our financial affairs. He had made the common mistake of believing you become an overnight millionaire as soon as you publish a book.

Ken and I had once thought this too, at least we had imagined that quite a considerable sum of money must follow the publication of a novel. In fact, most publishers daren't risk more than a 2000 print run of an unknown writer's first hardback. Many of these find their way into public libraries and my book had come into being before public lending rights for authors had seen the light of day.

In addition, and contrary to popular belief, it does not follow that after you have been published once everything you write will automatically get published. You have merely made one breakthrough and you're only as good as your last book. But how to try and convince the SS Bloodhound?

We had to show him bank statements and my savings book with approximately fifty pounds therein. I felt like telling him crossly that I did not have a fortune stashed away in a Swiss savings account, but with a great effort I held my tongue. He had totally spoiled the joy I had felt in having *Rhanna* published and I felt bleaker still when he promised (or was it threatened?) to return in a few months' time to review our situation. By then I would have received any royalties that were due to me.

Despite all this we sent him on his way fortified by tea and biscuits. Such is the strength of Highland hospitality, even though my father's temper boiled in my breast and I might have laced the Bloodhound's tea with arsenic had there been any in the house. We didn't even have rat poison!

5

First Christmas

A fortnight before Christmas we sneaked into the forest and cut down a beautiful little tree. Evelyn and I decked its boughs with tinsel and fairy lights, while Ken hung more lights round the front windows and put up a silver tree in Evelyn's room in order to silence the broad hints that she had been dropping since Hallowe'en.

We cut logs and piled them on the fire where they sizzled and hissed. Real live holly was gathered from the riverbank and placed round the pictures; Evelyn gathered pine cones till a huge basket of them stood on the hearth; vases were filled with hazel catkins and branches of evergreens.

Parcels came from my two sisters in far-off Australia, and every day the pile under the tree grew bigger. No one was forgotten. Jockey's cage was decorated with red tinsel which he pecked and picked but somehow never managed to pull apart. From an old Christmas card Evelyn cut a little red stocking which she strengthened with cardboard. This was hung inside his cage and for almost an hour he eyed it in a politely disinterested fashion. Then over he hopped to send it birling round with his beak. Thoroughly delighted with his new toy, he boxed and played with it and roared in a loud, bossy voice, 'Jockey's a comic' and, 'Evelyn did it!' The last was followed by a series of noises which got louder and ruder the more boisterous he became. She had never forgiven me for teaching him that, although she was gradually appreciating how funny the words sounded in his perky budgie voice. Anyway, she had gotten her own back by teaching him to say, 'Where's that cheeky, bad Chris?'

Honey seed bells were hung on the tree where they whirled round temptingly in front of his cage, making him hopping mad with frustration. To pacify him we gave him extra bits of millet, as Evelyn had strictly decreed that he was not to have a honey bell until Christmas morning.

Next on the scene was a net stocking full of doggie goodies which, being too heavy to suspend from the tree, was placed under it. At regular intervals, every day, Tania biffed it and poked it with her nose. She adored parcels of all descriptions and when any were brought into the house everything had to wait till she had made a thorough inspection. She would then supervise each item into its appropriate cupboard.

She knew the doggie stocking was for her, but made no attempt to pilfer anything. It was as if she knew she had to wait for the grand parcel-opening, and contented herself with daily, anticipatory sniffing sessions.

In the normal way of things, our kitchen was the coldest, most unwelcoming room in the house, with its condensation and its draughts and its numerous spidery gaps everywhere, but as the big day drew nearer it became filled with appetizing smells instigated by yours truly.

I had never been one to dabble in baking and cooking. All

my creative instincts had channelled themselves into other fields, yet, because I had always had to work with tight pursestrings, my ingenuity in culinary matters had somehow got me by in the kitchen.

If my way through life had been sprinkled with dazzling kitchens, I might perhaps have been more willing to spend my time over a hot stove. But there were several gourmet things at which I excelled. These had been instilled in me from the Govan days when Christmas and New Year meant homemade shortbread and black bun, and big juicy dumplings whose swollen breasts had fairly rattled the pan lids. I can still see Mam's face, flushed from the heat of the kitchen range whose glowing heart was never allowed to die, not even in summer when it was kept ticking over with damp dross. I can remember my big sister Kirsty, shutting herself in the scullery, there to make delicious concoctions of buttery tablet and tangy toffee on the gas stove, and – wonderful treat! – we were later allowed to lick sticky remains from wooden spoons and scrape sugary particles from the pans, though not before a good deal of squabbling with brothers and sisters to decide who should get what first.

Kirsty had always enjoyed baking and displayed a great deal of patience when it came to making fancy little cakes and scones, and though she shut herself away in the scullery to make some things she had to resign herself to rolling pastry on the kitchen table under our watchful eyes.

But we knew better than to make comment because being the eldest girl she was a law unto herself and would have thought nothing of taking a hefty spoon to our sticky fingers if the need arose. So, hardly daring to breathe, we looked on as she fashioned dough into wonderful shapes and made spicy buns packed with raisins and cinnamon and bits of peel. The clock ticked and hardly a sound was to be heard in the kitchen except for the rhythmic thump of the rolling pin or the clump of the wooden spoon in the big yellow mixing bowl.

I can still feel the pain of anticipation in my saliva glands as I watched and sniffed and kicked my brother Alec under the table for daring to sneak a wetted finger on to the tasty crumbs under his nose. If Kirsty took it into her head we would be sent packing into the room which would have been just too awful to bear.

In the end our silent vigil paid off. Oh, the joy of those first fluffy cakes straight out of the oven, falling apart at the first eager bite to release steam and fragrance before sweetness and delight pervaded the senses.

For days and days delicious aromas of baking and cooking saturated the kitchen, and now those same smells pervaded Polly Powdermill. The skills of mother and sister had passed on to me, and though it always took a good deal of persuasion to fire up my enthusiasm, Evelyn had plenty of such powers. With aching arms I mixed spicy dumplings and stirred big pans of golden, vanilla fudge. Evelyn watched and drooled at the mouth while beside her sat Tania, watching and drooling also. Since the kitchen was nice and warm from the heat of the calor gas stove, Jockey too was brought into the portals to sit in his cage atop the table and issue his own particular brand of instructions, with 'Jockey's a cheeky wee bugger' thrown in for good measure.

It was not beyond the realms of my imagination to picture the mice watching too, whiskers fairly quivering as they put their tiny paws together and prayed for lots of

Chistmassy crumbs. I could even see them performing a Highland fling, dressed in minute kilts, their festive table groaning under the weight of pilfered dumpling and mince pies. But I did not grudge them their crumbs. They were adorable little creatures, not the dun-coloured house variety, but field mice; soft, shy wee things with russet-coloured fur, big long whiskers and snuffly twitching pink noses.

Their summer world was of hedgerows and fields, mossy burrows and patches of warm sun where it was good to sit and have a wash, but the sun had dipped below Fraser's Hill, leaving the mill sunless and cold, so into barns and houses they came, seeking shelter from the winter weather.

We had been dismayed to lose the sun at the end of November. During spells of frost everything stayed white for days, gripped by penetrating cold that rimed the dead leaves in Stable Lane and glittered on the stark branches. Yet I grew to love those days of still and breathless frost. The wood smoke from the village drifted gently down to the river and hung suspended there among the trees, the sweet, tangy smell of it pervading the senses and making you love the winter countryside with all your heart.

Every morning I set out with Tania to gather my twigs for the fire and my frost-red nose fairly delighted in all the cold, sharp scents in the air. It was a joy to watch the blackbirds exploring the ground for insects, their beaks sending showers of dead leaves all round about; under my wheels brittle grasses and twigs crunched and snapped. It was pure happiness to pause for a while and look back to the smoke rising lazily from Polly Powdermill's chimney, and to know that when your fingertips got too sore and the drip at your nose too persistent you could go back home to the spit and sizzle of your yuletide fire.

But it wasn't all sweetness and light. The mornings brought dead ashes and a freezing house and a decided tendency to snuggle under the feathers for 'five minutes more'.

When the temperature sank below zero, Ken left a paraffin heater burning all night as we were always worried about keeping Jockey warm enough.

Even so, we often woke to ice *inside* the windows where condensation had frozen along the astragals. It took a good hour for the heat of a roaring fire to penetrate both sitting and living rooms and clear the ice away.

Just before Christmas, the pipe carrying our water supply from the hill froze up, and Ken had to lug buckets of water from further up the burn. We hadn't bargained for such an event, but in some strange way we took it in our stride and actually congratulated ourselves on the fact that, as we didn't have the usual water pipes in the house, we couldn't possibly suffer the inconvenience of a burst! You can always find something good in the worst situations.

Despite the suspended water supply and other inconveniences, Polly Powdermill *was* Christmas. There was a special quiet glow about it, and a magical sort of peace settled round it every evening when the fairy lights winked and the wood sang in the grate.

At that time we had no television and didn't want one. We simply grouped ourselves around the fire and indulged in our favourite hobbies. Ken made and painted beautiful models of steam engines in preparation for the day when he would have his own 'Railway Room'. I knitted Aran suits and jumpers and painted pictures in both chalk and oil pastels. Evelyn read, or drew her big, clumpy birds, and fashioned the most intricate patterns on paper which she later coloured with felt pens.

Quite often we managed to tear ourselves away from the fire and, wrapping up warmly, we took Tania for walks in the moonlight. The air was sharp and freezing cold and because there were no street lamps there was no annoying glare to detract from the spellbinding sight of black hills etched against a sky ablaze with millions of stars.

Brig O'Doon was enchanting in the moonlight. Orange lights winked warmly from the windows, trails of wood smoke drifted to meet the vapoury mist rising from the river.

In the stillness it was possible to hear a dog barking from a farm miles along the glen; once or twice we heard the gruff bark of a fox echoing in the corries of the hills. Sometimes there was the grunt of deer in the woods and, of course, the hoot and toot of the owls from the trees.

How lovely it was to wander along and hear the cold plish-plash of a tumbling burn and to watch the moon rising above the hills till the silent countryside was bathed in its silvery light.

Then it was bed, good and warm and safe, and deep sleep and dreamings till morning lit the eastern sky with rosy blushes and you snuggled down for that precious few minutes before the bustle of a new day began.

The persistent but welcome 'Brrrr!' from the Teasmade was followed by Tania's cold, wet nose questing in under the quilt to shiver your spine before it was followed by a warm, moist tongue kissing you thoroughly awake.

This affectionate awakening set off a chain of family events.

'EVELYN! Wakey, wakeeee!'

My dulcet tones rent the air, causing my still-slumbering spouse to open one bleary eye and mutter, 'Whasatime?' before burrowing himself deeper into the depths of the blankets to go where no man has gone before. How he avoided suffocation will forever remain a mystery to me, but even supposing he had been possessed of the ability to turn himself outside in, he could never escape the morning avalanche of female bodies upon his person.

Up Tania would jump to flatten his feet; in Evelyn would march to fill her cup from the Teasmade and plump herself down beside Tania. When, groaning and moaning, he managed to extricate himself from layers of ensnaring flesh, up he would heave himself to hold out his hand weakly for his first cuppy of the day. And there upon the bed we would all sip and yawn and not look too much at one another, for none of us were morning people, not even Evelyn who had to have her engines fired before she could get going, nor Tania, too, for that matter. Once she had nipped outside for a quick piddle and had partaken of her cornflakes, she liked nothing better than to sneak back into the bedroom for a long lie.

It is amazing how the passing of one hour can so completely change a domestic scene. In the space of that time we were all up, the fire was lit, breakfast made and eaten, Evelyn was waiting at the door for the bus and Jockey, freed from his protective nightly layers, was doing headstands on his perch and from between his legs was telling the wild birds outside the window that he was a comic, then adding knowingly, 'Jockey's a budgie.'

Then it was Christmas morning, the Wee Comic was

pecking happily at his honey bell and Tania, who had waited patiently for the parcel-opening ceremony to begin, was sprawled among the wrappings, her nose buried deep in her doggie stocking. In her enthusiasm she had got it well and truly stuck, and she was waving the stocking in the air like a big, extra, knobbly net nose.

Rescue restored her dignity and rewarded her with choc drops, and while she and Jockey were enjoying their spoils the wild birds were going wilder still over their own special Christmas treat.

I regularly made fat-cakes for the bird table but today I had made an especially big and tasty one that contained seeds, chopped bacon, crumbs, oatmeal, lentils and split peas. When set this was nailed to the table as, from experience, we knew that the blackbirds could knock it to the ground where it would become a tasty titbit for marauding cats and other creatures.

Different bird species had different fads, so as well as the cake we hung nuts for the tits, spread oats for Robin Redbreast and breadcrumbs for the finches.

Ken put slices of bread and potato halves out in the field for the magpies, jays and the crows, in order to keep them busy. The crows in particular had a habit of divebombing the blackbirds, to make them drop any food they might be carrying. We had learned to save them leftovers of stale bread and potatoes so that the smaller birds would get peace at the bird table. But we loved those big, beautiful birds, Ken having a particular fondness for the crows with their struttings and sly strategies, and we watched out for them in the bare winter trees, and for the flashes of black and white that heralded the arrival of the magpies. The jays you could always hear coming, garrulously calling to one another in the woodland till you were rewarded with a sight of them, pink-buff birds with distinctive blue and black barring on the wing edges.

The animals fed and happy it was the turn of the humans, and off I went to collect Gran and bring her back for Christmas dinner. We made merry with crackers and paper hats and a good dram or two which further loosened her tongue, for she could blether could Gran, and take a good laugh. Then it was home to bed, contented and happy, even though she had lost again at cards for which she always came armed with a Smartie tube filled with pennies.

It had been a lovely first Christmas at Polly Powdermill. Dry, freezing cold weather yet not cold enough to freeze the water supply; no rain on the roof – or rather, inside the roof; a good old-fashioned sort of Christmas with no TV to detract from the simple pleasures of chatter and family games, carols on the radio, and the joys to be found round a cosy hearth.

Outside the windows the stars winked, the tree glowed with a special kind of glow; Jockey's tired little yellow head was under his wing; Tania snored contentedly on the rug; Evelyn's sleepy voice came from her room, quietly singing herself to sleep with a rather flat rendering of 'Rudolph'.

Polly Powdermill wrapped us round with peace and warmth and love that came from deep within the spirit of the little house.

'The house is happy with us,' I sighed dreamily, 'I can feel it all around.'

'Me too,' Ken whispered back, taking my hand and clasping it warmly. 'It's been a special Christmas.'

We said nothing more for a while. The clock ticked lazily, the house dozed and dreamed. I wanted to stay there forever, warm by the fire, savouring the glittering night beyond the window; the shimmer of the fairy lights; Ken's hand in mine.

A soft little snore issued through the silence. Christmas day was over, the night waited for human creatures to be abed as was the natural order of things. Everything was back to normal.

6

Winter Wonderland

January brought the snow, big, fat, fluffy flakes that whirled down, blotting out the hills and the trees, gradually blocking the road. Mill Brae was bad enough in ice and frost but in snow it could be treacherous. The volume of traffic grew less and less till finally there was none, and we were alone in a smothering world, cocooned in the tiny oasis that was Polly Powdermill.

Our water had once more frozen and both Ken and Evelyn had quite a job slithering over the snowbound road to fetch it from the burn. It was then we learned the truth of the saying, 'You never miss the water till the well runs dry.' Our hard-won icy water, sitting in pails in the kitchen, became a very precious commodity indeed, and was used only for cooking and tea-making. For washing up and other such tasks, snow was scooped into pans and pails and any other receptacle that hadn't been commandeered for the loft. When the dishes were done the water was saved and sluiced down the toilet pan. Not a drop was wasted. Each morning the hot water bottles were emptied into a basin to be used for smalls and other sundries, including ourselves. From sheer necessity we three quickly learned to be extremely frugal and soon became experts at washing large areas of anything, including human flesh, with minute portions of water.

Woe betide anyone who unthinkingly flushed the cludge after Ken had painstakingly filled the cistern 'for emergencies'. It was so natural to pull that little handle and whoosh! A couple of gallons of water went literally down the drain, and you sat there wishing you could go with it rather than face the music. But there were times when we all forgot.

Everything was muffled and rather eerie as the whirling snow grew thicker and heavier, and a freezing wind piled it into drifts till we couldn't see the fence that divided us from the field. We had our own whiteout there in the glen and without even the postman paying his usual calls we felt cut off from the rest of the world. But life had to go on in our small sphere, though, with the shops being shut over the festive period, we hadn't had much opportunity to stock up our sadly depleted larder.

Marilla Mini had completely disappeared under a snow blanket, the only indication of its presence outside our bedroom window being a domed lump, appreciably higher than the surrounding drifts.

How strange it was to open the east door each morning to be met by a wall of snow higher than my wheels. So deep was the silence it was possible to hear the whisper of snowflakes against the window panes. The only signs of life in the virginal fields were patterns of footprints made by wild creatures that had wandered the night. We were enthralled by these manifestations of life and it became a fascinating game to try and guess the identities of the animals that had made them.

Some led right up to the door and zigzagged away again, a mouse perhaps, questing for food and shelter in a landscape that seemed to offer neither. Others were round and quite big and these we knew belonged to a white cat who lived wild in the woods and who slept in the old sheds beside our house. Since first sighting this poor abandoned creature we had left scraps of food and saucers of milk inside the ruins of the changing shed. We could only hope she would receive the benefits in a highly competitive animal kingdom.

Most of the prints were tiny and easily identified as belonging to the smaller mammals, others were bigger and clumpier and might have been made by Evelyn's bird caricatures. We guessed that they might have been made by moles with their wonderfully big pale feet.

Deeper marks came from the roe deer whom we often glimpsed browsing amongst the trees; dog-like tracks made us think of a fox; smaller, five-toed versions could have come from a stoat or a weasel.

The most prolific tracks came from the birds, all criss-crossing one another with here and there the scumble of a blackbird's floundering wing. The bird table was half buried but we cleared the window ledges and shared what we had with robins, tits, finches, blackbirds and – great surprise – the occasional wren popping in among the rest to snatch a crumb or two.

Jockey went daft with delight as he watched all the comings and goings, the flutterings and the scufflings, and he listened with interest to the scoldings and fightings and Robbie's tic, tic, coming from the branches of the rowan tree.

'Where's the burdies?' I asked him each day and very soon he was shouting the same question, the minute his night wrappings came off, in a very broad Glasgow accent which didn't deter the wild 'burdies' outside the window.

But while Jockey was pleased enough with his lot, Tania was not in the least amused by the blizzards which robbed her of her beloved walks and made the task of going outside to relieve herself a very hazardous affair indeed. Out she would venture, muffled to the ears in snow, upon which she would hastily squat to make a small, steaming vent, before paddling back up to the house to settle herself by the fire, there to gnaw an ancient bone or join Evelyn in her room to play tunnels with the bed covers.

Yet, snow was Tania's natural element. Her ancestors had travelled the Siberian wastes with the Samoyede nomads, guarding their reindeer herds, sleeping with them in their tents, sharing their meagre food supplies of raw, dried fish, and occasionally, out of sheer necessity, themselves becoming food for their masters. The Samoyede people treasured their dogs and only fed on their edible flesh as a desperate last resort.

Some of the old ways are still inherent in the present-day Samoyed dog. They can fend for themselves in the wild if need be, but they also adore human beings and love nothing better than to share a human bed – inside the blankets with their head on a pillow, if their owners are mugs enough to let them get away with it.

Shona, our first darling Samoyed, without any training whatsoever, had been an expert at rounding up cattle, as she proved to us several times when we had started off married life in a farm cottage. She had been little more than a pup when she had left our side to go tearing over the fields, and though we shouted ourselves hoarse she didn't falter till she had herded the young bullocks into a tight knot, never once nipping a single heel in the process. Then and only then had she come creeping back to us wearing a suitably hangdog expression. Ever after, whenever the opportunity presented itself, she was away over the fields, obeying her instincts as she rounded up cattle like a well-trained sheepdog.

For a dog of her size she had never had a big appetite, often going without food for a day or two, again a throw-back to days when food was scarce and often non-existent.

The same could not be said for Tania. She adored food and gulped up anything that came her way, even apple cores and peanuts. If the birds dropped bread she pounced on it with a grateful smile; she crunched mint Tic-tacs and Polo mints with huge enjoyment; she stole pieces of apple and orange and tasty crusts of brown bread from Jockey's cage, but wasn't daft enough to do it if there was anyone about, and for a long time I wondered where the titbits were going.

At first I thought that, as well as owning a gourmet dog, I also had a very greedy bird on my hands, one who could swallow lumps of fruit in one go and still manage to maintain a normal budgie size.

Then one day I came into the living room during the perpetration of the foul deed. At least she had the grace to look thoroughly ashamed and cowed and was so upset at being found out she dropped the filched piece of apple on to the carpet and slunk and cowered in abject shame, the whites of her eyes showing as she turned her drooping head away from me.

Jockey, who had obviously enjoyed every moment of his furry pal's nose questing around his cage, was gleefully shouting, 'Hallo Tania, give us a cuddle!' and so quaint was the scene I burst out laughing, much to Tania's relief, though she was too sensitive at that moment to even begin to try and make amends and went slinking behind the couch to nurse her wounded pride in solitude.

But the tempting goodies stuck into the spars of the bird's cage were always too much for her, and after that day, if we wanted to have a bit of fun with her, one or other of us would come into the living room at the crucial moment and catch her at it.

She soon learned to make a game of it and after the initial and obligatory slinkings and creepings she would wag her tail and everything else until her entire body became one big fluffy unit of grins and grunts and 'please can I have that measly bit of fruit now?' expression in her twinkly brown eyes.

But many of the things Shona had loved, Tania loved also; mainly humans and anything connected with them, their knees, their noses, their sweaty feet, their beds and their funny, pink ears. Tania was an expert on ears. Forbye loving to wash them she adored nibbling the lobes and it was the most spine-tingling sensation to feel those great, glistening white teeth gently caressing and pecking and never once nipping.

And, like Shona, she loved ice, to break frozen puddles, to crunch it and crackle it with her teeth, to lick it and suck it and pull big icicles from walls and gutters and hold them between her paws and slobber over them for all the world like a child with an ice lolly.

And most of all she loved the snow. For two days and nights it billowed over the landscape. Then it stopped, and the countryside around Polly Powdermill was a winter wonderland. Fronds of evergreens bowed low to the ground with the weight of their snow blankets, delicate shrubs wore shawls of lacy white while the branches of rowans, oaks, sycamores and other deciduous trees made sparkling traceries against the deep blue of the sky. The quiet grey of the mill ruins poked through undulating white quilts, walls and fences were half buried in drifts, overhead telephone wires were feathery ropes stretching away into cold infinity.

Into this glistening land Tania ran, barking, dancing, making tunnels with her nose till a miniature snow mountain rose up in front of her eyeballs. She rolled in it, dug it, buried her muzzle in it, and ate it, and while all this was going on Ken and Evelyn got to work with spades and I did my bit with the coal shovel.

The wild birds were overjoyed to welcome us into their world, they came hopping and slithering to meet us, down over the rooftops, out from the bushes, the bracken, the branches. Tania and her antics didn't worry them in the least. The birds were used to her poking and sniffing round the bird table and had become quite cheeky and daring in her presence.

But it was Robbie Redbreast I loved best, perched shy and aloof on a fence post, his breast a red blaze against the white backcloth, the tips of his brown coat tails touching the snow dumpling of his perch, his bowings and flirtings and distinctive 'tic, tic, tic' telling me to hurry up with his breakfast.

For him I always kept a special supply of porridge oats and when Ken and Evelyn had unearthed the bird table, and the other birds were feeding and squabbling, I cleared a patch of ground for Robbie so that he could eat his oats in peace.

It is a myth that robins are aggressive and quarrelsome. For years I had observed their habits and knew that they only fought with their own kind – and then only if it was another cock. Females were well tolerated and allowed into the territory, often being permitted to feed first, even out of the breeding season.

Robins shyly hold back at the bird table and are easily chased away by the bolder chaffs and blackies, so they wait until the coast is clear before coming in for a snatched meal. As a result, they are often out of luck through waiting so long. That was why I fed my robins in places well away from other birds and I had succeeded in making friends with a succession of redbreasts.

At our last house, a dear fluffy little robin had regularly hopped over the doorstep whenever I opened the door. He had shown no fear of me and on several occasions he had made for the bedroom, there to flutter up on the dressing table and look at himself critically and calmly in the mirror before getting down and hopping unhurriedly back out of the door to peck at the oats I had scattered for him.

When I found him dead at my door one wintry morning, I realized he had been an old bird who had, in some strange way, wanted to share his last days with a human pal.

How sad that their lives are so brief. They always look so alert and vibrant, yet in the space of little more than a year they live, breed and die, providing some predator, or a speeding car, doesn't get them first. I've lost count of the number of dead robins I have seen on our busy roads.

The paths cleared I was able to move about in my chair, and we all set to, to build a giant snowman, complete with coal eyes, a long, carrot nose, a woolly scarf and bunnet and a homemade broom under his arm.

When finally he stood there in all his splendour and we

66

were gazing at him with pride and admiration, Tania suddenly leapt up and stole his nose. Off she bounded over the field, her trophy held firm in her teeth.

She pranced, she danced, she threw the carrot up in the air, over and over, each time catching it in her grinning jaws. She barked at it, she played peever with it and then seeing Ken and Evelyn hot on her heels she was off again, a silvery blur, and the barkings and laughings of them all rang and rang in the sharp clean air.

Soon after that the water came back on, the snow plough and the grit lorry between them reopened the road, and the postman's rounds returned to normal. But it was a cold, snowy January. Hoar frost held the glen in an icy grip, making travel a hazardous affair. It snowed and thawed and snowed and froze. The roof of the cottage groaned under its snowy mass, which, every time there was a thaw, slid down over the eaves to create a snow canopy dripping with icy fangs. Ken became so worried about the burden on our fragile roof he clambered up on to it, and, with the aid of a brush, pushed off as much of the freezing blanket as he was able to reach.

The water regularly froze and unfroze, but the sun had come back to the mill and this made us feel much more cheerful about everything and better able to carry on with our lives without too many grumbles.

Since the living and sitting rooms ran into one another, with continual traffic to and from the kitchen, there was no separate room I could use as a study, so Ken set up a table for me in the living room near the fire. There I wrote the last chapters of the second Rhanna book, *Rhanna at War*, and painted pictures in readiness for the art show which was held annually in Dunoon. These were mainly paintings of local scenes and were very popular with American families attached to the nearby Holy Loch naval base. I also got on with various pastel paintings for which I had been commissioned, and, at the request of Blond & Briggs, I started on the artwork for the cover of *Rhanna at War*.

How I ever got through so much work in such unsuitable conditions, I'll never know, but my creativity was at fever pitch and I think I would have been able to write and paint even if I had been living in a cave in the wilderness.

If Ken hadn't been at home, tending to fires and water and numerous other household tasks, I might never have achieved what I did, but he cooked and cleaned and saw to everything. However, he couldn't protect me from the usual callers, and very often my train of thought would be rudely interrupted so that I found it difficult to concentrate my entire mind on my literary outpourings.

When Evelyn came home from school everything had to be cleared away so that the family could have the use of the living area in the evenings.

It was a tiresome business, continually having to set up my things, but the determination I had inherited from my mother was strong within me; that, coupled with the stubbornness passed on to me from my father, somehow drove me on.

As well as everything else, I also had to deal with fan mail. This was a spin-off from writing that I hadn't bargained for, but as each day passed more and more letters arrived, all telling me how much *Rhanna* had been enjoyed and asking, would there be more books about the little Hebridean island?

Oh yes! There would be more. I wrote back with the news that the second novel was nearing completion and glowed with appreciation for these wonderfully complimentary letters. They spurred me on to write and write and I will always be grateful to those people who took the time and trouble to put pen to paper. Many of them had never before done such a thing and a lot of the letters began: 'This is the first time I have ever written to an author...'

When my spirits were at a low ebb I would get out my letters and read them all over again and marvel anew that out there, in the big, wide world, were people who laughed and cried over my books and so loved the characters that one woman wrote: 'I never wanted to come to the end but now I have and I'm pining for the next book – and the next...'

7

Wee, Cowering, Timorous Beasties

Another boost came in the middle of February of that year. My belated advance on publication of *Rhanna* arrived from my publishers, the grand amount of £250, and when Saturday came we all went into Dunoon for a little shopping spree which included much-needed shoes for Evelyn.

On arrival home there was a letter waiting from Hutchinsons. Bob Cowan had sent them the first volume of my autobiography, *Blue Above the Chimneys*, and they wanted to publish it. I could hardly believe it. First the advance, now this. Normally, I am your typical undemonstrative Scot (bottling it all up, unable to let go), but when I read that letter I bubbled over with joy and, letting out a shout of pure abandon, I grabbed both Evelyn and Ken and kissed them soundly.

Ken was delighted. It was he who had encouraged me to write about my Govan upbringing and of my hospital experiences, and, though I had eventually succumbed to his persuasions and had produced an enormous tome about my tenement childhood, I had gradually lost interest in it when various publishers had said it would need drastic pruning to make it work.

I had pruned it so much it hurt, had then been told it was 'lively and readable' but still needed cutting, and after that I had shoved it out of sight and had all but forgotten it. But Ken never had. He had spoken to Bob Cowan about it and, after reading it, Bob had sent it to Hutchinsons for their perusal.

And now the result of all that was here in my hand, which fairly trembled with excitement...But there was a snag – there usually is when you are a new, raw, inexperienced writer as I was then. The manuscript needed a final polishing, the rough edges smoothed away, but so buoyant was I that none of that mattered. I decided to rewrite the entire thing once more, and in no way was I to be interrupted while doing so. So Ken set me up at the living room window. The little Imperial Good Companion I had inherited from Dad Cameron was placed upon the ledge, together with jotters and pens, typing paper and copy paper and all the other bits and pieces necessary to a writer.

The window ledge was cramped and cold, draughts blew in on my knees from the badly fitting sashes, but a hot water bottle made life a bit easier, and anyway, the window afforded a fine view of the fields and hills and anything was better than sitting in the middle of the living room in everyone's way.

From morning till night my fingers flew over the keyboard. I was so busy and lost in thought I barely saw the view in front of me, nor was I really aware of anything going on in the house. My eyes were to the hills, my back to the family, and in my mind I was back in Govan, the colour of it, the shabbiness, the backcourts teeming with snot-nosed children, the rag and bone man heralding his arrival with a blast of a tinny horn. Mam and Da, brothers and

71

sisters, pranks in the park and capers in the cludge, Hallowe'en and Christmas and candy floss at the shows in Glasgow Green.

It was all there, bouncing out from my fingers, the laughter, the tears, the joys, the sadnesses. After an hour or so of sitting there my hands were frozen, my feet blocks of ice, but I kept on typing, typing, hardly aware of physical discomforts.

As the days wore on my ears became attuned to something else other than the clackety-clack of my typewriter. At first I had only a vague sense of something unusual going on in the vicinity of the ledge, but so lost was I in my own little world I paid scant attention to anything else.

It was only during interludes of deep thought, when I would sit back and gaze abstractedly at the burns tumbling down the hills, that an awareness of slight rustlings and tiny squeaks penetrated my consciousness.

It was Tania who confirmed that I wasn't hearing things. She had a habit of lying peacefully beside my chair when I was working, but she had been alert of late, sitting up and listening, ears pricked, head cocked to one side, her tongue held in her mouth so that only the pink tip showed.

After a day or two of this, I called on Ken to come and listen also. But, as is the way of things, the rustlings immediately stopped when he came near, and after a few moments of impatient listening he rushed away to attend to more important matters.

But soon after, when he was trying to seal up the gaps under the sill in an effort to stop the draughts, he too heard the sounds. 'It couldn't be mice,' was his verdict. 'They would never hang around here with all the din you make.'

So we left it for a while, but eventually curiosity got the better of us and one day we shifted all my things to allow Ken gently to prise up the ledge. Breath held, we peeked inside the resulting space and there, in amongst lathe and plaster, was the cosiest little field mouse nest, made up of dry grass, wood shavings, leaves, and a good tuft or two of Tania's fluffy white hairs.

'Will I get rid of it?' Ken asked but in a tone that suggested his unwillingness to destroy a creation that must have cost the little creatures weeks of sweated labour.

He knew of course what my answer would be. The ledge was carefully fixed back into place and to the accompaniment of furtive scrapings beneath my typewriter work on *Blue Above the Chimneys* carried on, not to mention the completion of *Rhanna at War*, and letters to publishers and fans.

On uninterrupted days I often wrote from eleven in the morning till eleven at night, and would crawl to my bed tired out but unable to sleep for all my book characters marching through my mind, not to mention plots and story-lines for future books.

You have to be totally dedicated, determined, and thoroughly single-minded to write a book. You have to have guts, mental strength and the type of spiritual stamina that transcends physical frailties.

You also have to be prepared to spend many solitary hours with your eyes glued to jotters and paper, which may or may not get filled depending on the strength of your muse and the extent of your imagination. You must also be prepared to sign away the joy of reading other people's books for pure pleasure only.

Research takes up an immense amount of any spare time you might have, and you must bury your nose into books you might not really care for but which are the means of providing the facts and the information necessary to make your work authentic. I soon found out that people simply adore pulling you up for an inaccuracy, even though it might be a very minor, incorrect detail.

You must lock yourself away from the real world, and throw away the key, until only mind-shattering fatigue and physical exhaustion forces you to put down the pen. And after all that you can only hope and pray that your efforts have not been in vain, and that you just might get your work published.

You also have to make time to keep in touch with friends and relatives, or you might find yourself distanced from both, and if you have a husband and children, the quality of the time you spend with them is even more important. So, difficult though it was, we had friends in, we went to our local art club once a week, we went to Gran's for tea. We had her up to the cottage for dinner and a game of gin rummy, and the number of pennies in her Smartie tube went down rapidly. On one memorable occasion she won hands down and went home walking on air, looking for all the world as if she had just won the football pools.

All through that winter Evelyn regularly came home crawling with cold germs, 'Germans' as Da had called them, roaring with laughter at his own wit and displaying not a jot of sympathy for the victim of the 'invasion'. With a fire burning cheerily in her grate, off to bed Evelyn was packed to nurse her Germans in solitude, or maybe to read, or draw her clumpy birds if she felt up to it.

Nothing diminished her appetite, however. She ate large

amounts of food after which she would make out she hadn't been all *that* hungry. Ken would laugh and suggest that maybe she had a starving army of warriors hiding under her bed, German or otherwise.

Meantime, her germs gleefully and viciously attached themselves to me to render me voiceless, breathless, and devoid of any appetite, though seldom did they land me in bed. Like Da, I just wouldn't lie down to illness as I always felt worse under the blankets.

Ken on the other hand, though slim as a yardstick, hardly ever succumbed to such miseries, and while both Evelyn and I sneezed and croaked our way through the winter, he flew around the house as usual, keeping the home fires burning.

In between colds, we helped him to knock down what remained of the ruin that had been attached to the west gable, and it was the greatest of fun to wield a hammer, getting rid of any frustrations in the process, though not without a feeling of sadness on my part as I was wont to pause and think of the time when people had laughed and talked within the walls we were demolishing with such carefree abandon.

Ken, being the ingenious soul he is, left a small portion of a back wall still standing and, with the addition of a few bricks, built a little raised flower bed where I could plant my spring seeds.

The advance I had received for *Rhanna* went towards the cost of building a concrete patio area on this west side of the house, and when it was finished it was a treat to sit there as the days grew longer and warmer.

The frogs had laid their spawn in the roadside ditches during February and a few blobs of it had found their way into the old cast iron bathtub. Evelyn had gotten her way over the tadpoles!

She and I also kept some in jars inside the house. I had never grown out of the thrill of watching the growth and development of living things. As a child in Govan I had picked daisies and kept them in egg cups so that I could observe their pink-tipped petals closing as they 'went to sleep for the night'. I had planted seeds in Da's window boxes and had waited with the utmost impatience for the tiny seedlings to appear. The old man and I had shared that love of growing things, and it was from him I learned to differentiate between weeds and flowers. He often allowed a bunch of chickweed to grow, because he said the wild birds liked it and would come to the window to pick it. That was Da, hard and tough about so many things, soft and tender about birds and flowers, a light in his eye when he recounted a well-worn tale about reviving a half-dead canary he had once owned by trickling a tiny amount of brandy down its little throat.

What a pity he had only briefly known the joys of a garden in the housing scheme we had moved to from Govan. He would have been in his element in a garden, would Da, with an aviary thrown in for good measure. If he had been born privileged he might have been so many things he wasn't. The circumstances of anyone's beginnings must influence their outlook to some extent, although a rotten environment doesn't have to lead to rotten behaviour. Good will out if it's there in the first place, and, though Da's upbringing had made him as hard as nails, he was basically a good man who tried his best to instil his own strict code of morals in his children.

Both he and Mam would have loved our glen. It was rich

with teeming life and my enthusiasm for everything that the countryside nurtured matched my daughter's. She had always had a knack for finding interesting things, and these she would bring home for me to study, be it an abandoned bird's nest or pieces of egg shell, or beautiful stones she had found in the river shallows, and we were both delighted to discover the frog spawn.

I loved watching the little round eggs stretching out into elongated black bean shapes, which moved about in their protective spheres like embryos in a womb.

And all around us the daffodils were bursting, great clumps of them in the fields and in amongst the mill ruins, masses of them in our garden.

Ken was now busy at the warm east side of the house, building another patio area and a concrete ramp leading from the door so that at last I could get in and out instead of merely sitting in the doorway gazing out on the mill policies. It was warm and sheltered there, because of the high, surrounding wall, and on sunny days, having finished typing both *Rhanna at War* and the newly revised *Blue Above the Chimneys*, I sat with my jotters and in longhand started work on a novel set in a gunpowder mill one hundred years ago.

With the coming of spring the mice moved out of the house, and now we only glimpsed them in the grass as they darted out of cover to nab a crumb or two that had dropped from the bird table. Most of the birds, except for the opportunist chaffinches, had deserted us as the skies grew wider and the days grew longer. They were all busy, flirting and courting and building nests, and it was a wonderful sight to watch the male wagtails during their courtship displays and to see them bobbing and dipping over the rooftops as they searched for insects.

A group of sheep who had wandered the mill all winter gave birth to lambs in the field behind our house, and Tania was fascinated by these tiny white babies. We often wondered if she thought they were Samoyed pups, as, without any wicked intent whatsoever, she would sneak up to a sleeping lamb and just sit staring at it, utterly entranced, making no attempt to touch it or waken it in any way. This went on day after day, until one old ewe espied her beside her lamb and without more ado Tania was given a terrible walloping. Over and over the ewe viciously butted her, grunting belligerently all the while, and up to the house Tania came flying, her tail tucked between her legs, a most hurt and bewildered expression on her face.

After that she had to content herself with peeping at the lambs from the safety of a bush or grassy tussock, although, when the lambs grew bigger and bolder and would cheekily gambol up to her, she simply could not resist the urge to wash their faces before their mothers sent her packing with a few raucous bleats.

They also bestowed on her something else she hadn't bargained for – ticks! This was one category of wildlife I did not like to see living and growing. I hated and abhorred the disgusting brutes with all my heart though not until coming to live at Polly Powdermill had I encountered them in such vast numbers, and in all our years of living at the mill I developed such an aversion towards them it almost amounted to tick-phobia.

I discovered them on Tania one morning whilst she was gracefully ensconced beside me on the bed. After one glance at the tiny, black, spidery-like creatures, crawling in and out of her white fur, I recoiled in horror. Only once before had I parted so hastily with the feathers, and that had been when a wasp had gotten into our bedroom, to crawl under the blankets and sting me on a part of my anatomy that ensured I couldn't sit comfortably for days. But at least a wasp had the decency to let go after the perpetration of its foul deed, not so a tick who clung and sucked and swelled in a most revolting manner.

Divebombing into my chair I opened my mouth and gave my lungs full throttle.

'Ticks!' I yelled and wouldn't have cared if the postman himself had come galloping in to the rescue. 'Millions of ticks! Bloody bags of bloody blood!'

Well of course it wasn't the postman who came rushing in to eye me with questioning surprise, it was Ken, his hands all sooty from cleaning out the fire.

'Look, look,' I gasped, backing away from Tania and her ticks as if both she and them were about to leap on me at any moment.

One glance and Ken bundled poor, bewildered Tania off the bed and out of the door and outside she remained till I was up and dressed and able to view the situation with just mild hysteria.

But I had always been able to steel myself for most domestic crises and I did so now, if only to save my beloved dog the fate of being shut out of doors for the rest of the summer.

Out to her I went, armed with paper hankies and a bottle of disinfectant, and with pieces of tissue soaked in the same I one by one extracted the little blighters, hoping the disinfectant would instantly asphyxiate them.

But I soon made the discovery that the tiny bloodsuckers did not succumb so easily. As large as life they crawled in amongst the debris of tissues and calling on Ken for matches

I set fire to them then and there and thoroughly revelled in watching their cremation.

Tania sat patiently throughout the entire operation, never even flinching when the hankies went up in flames and even lazily shutting her eyes as she allowed me to explore her coat.

From puppyhood she had loved being handled. In those days she would bite and play with comb or brush but now she would lie back and go to sleep, only glancing up sheepishly if the brush went too near her private parts when a look on her face said all too plainly, 'Hey, go easy back there, those bristles are sharp.'

I only needed to say 'up, Tania' and she would obligingly heave herself round to enable me to work on her other side.

So all through the tick-removing session she was as good as gold and later, when the really unsavoury part of the proceedings got underway, that of removing the disgusting little bags of blood that were attached to her skin by touching them with a lit cigarette in order to make them release their grip, she barely flinched, trusting me implicitly not to burn her. Though Ken loved animals he had never been good at working with them and so it was left to me that day to relieve Tania of her visitors.

Evelyn, on the other hand, was wonderful. From an early age she had cleaned up animal waste matter without flinching, and when she came home from school she employed herself helping me to get rid of the remaining horrors, and I think she really enjoyed hearing them pop as she bore them to the grate for burning.

That of course was not the end of the matter. Tania went on picking up ticks on her long coat and we went on picking them out, using sheep dip, paraffin, and anything else we could think of to make them release their fangs from Tania's tender skin, all the while hoping that those same fangs would never get an opportunity to dig themselves into *our* flesh.

Then one day we had a visit from a lady who had spent a lot of her life in Africa and who was idly fondling our dog when her eyes suddenly lit up.

'Ticks!' she exclaimed and I fancied she was delighted by the discovery. 'We used to spend our evenings in Africa picking ticks from our dogs.'

So saying she held Tania between her knees to twist out the ticks with expertise and bung them into the fire. No disinfectant, no sheep dip, no glowing cigarette ends, just a twist and a pull and a few mini explosions from the fire.

After that we bought a tick collar to fasten around Tania's throat. It never quite solved the problem but it did relieve it to some degree though darling, darling Tania, who loved beds and pillows and luxuriously comfortable long lie-ins, was never to know that privilege for the rest of the summer and the expression of hurt and accusation upon her face on being relegated to the kitchen regions at night was something I had to turn my own face away from or I could never have resisted the appeal in those big, moist, beseeching brown eyes.

8

The Wee Comic

Jockey, too, had his share of adventures that summer. When the weather grew warmer Ken fixed a hook to the underside of the little awning over the east door. On this hook Jockey swung gently in his cage, his initial awe of the great outdoors wearing off rapidly.

He soon got to know the ropes and whenever he was being transported out to his hook he would screech and flutter with the utmost anticipation.

We of course fixed a light cover over one half of his cage so that the sun wouldn't beat directly on to him. Under this airy canopy he rattled through his vast vocabulary, his Glasgow accents growing richer and broader whenever the wild birds came near.

At first they cocked beady eyes at him as if to say, 'Who is this feathered nut with the human voice?' but they soon grew used to him hanging there, swearing and talking at them, and one chaffinch grew so bold he often hopped up on the cage to peck away at the pieces of millet stuck into the spars. When this happened Jockey almost turned head over heels with delight and he would bob rapidly up and down, his body and head feathers fluffed out till he looked like Tweety Pie of cartoon fame.

Villagers from Brig O'Doon, walking by on the other side of the wall, were enthralled when the patter of this amazing budgie reached their ears, and they would go on their way smiling, cries of 'give us a kiss' and 'Evelyn did it, rasp, rasp', following them down the brae.

The Wee Comic's fame was rapidly spreading. Gran often came for afternoon tea accompanied by a crony. Beside the cage they would arrange themselves, Gran holding her breath in case all her boasting about Jockey's prowess might rebound on her, for if he was moulting, or just not in the mood, he would dig his little yellow head under his wing and mutter sullenly to himself, impervious to all coaxings.

On the first occasion this was exactly what happened, with a most uncooperative budgie sourly surveying the big human faces peering into his domain.

Tea was dispensed and eaten and the visitors were about to depart when he shook himself, fluffed himself up, and launched into action.

Both Gran and her friend were enthralled. As well as his usual chatter he threw in a few more phrases he had recently learned; he made a perfect imitation of me drawing in my breath as I spoke to him and another of the living room handle being turned and the door creaking open, both latter sounds tricking the family so successfully, we had all, at one time or another, come out of various rooms at various times to see who was entering our house.

For Gran and her delighted pal he gave a wonderful performance and a grand finale of juicy raspberries, one upon the other, rolling off his tongue with the greatest of ease.

When the visitors reached the door he yelled fiendishly,

'Grannie's a dinner!' and fell off his perch with excitement.

The next time Gran came she brought with her a minister who had for years been a family friend. All through tea, with its accompanying clatter and chatter, Jockey talked his head off and no one paid him the slightest attention, though both Ken and I, our ears attuned to everything the little guy had to say, no matter the distraction of other sounds, looked at one another and with our eyes sent signals that said we hoped he wouldn't swear, 'Not in front of the minister!'

Then came the inevitable lull in the conversation and as clear as a crystal bell and as loud as it could possibly be 'Jockey's a cheeky wee bugger!' boomed forcibly into the silence, followed by the rudest, wettest imitations of the most graceless of human sounds, the kind one hopes will never be heard by any ears except our own.

Gran's jaw fell open and, trying to look very prim and proper, she sipped her tea with one finger daintily crooked and almost choked in the effort of holding back her mirth.

But the minister was a man of the world, his eyes twinkled, he chuckled and giggled and craned his neck to look with admiration at Tweety Pie in his cage, a picture of perfect innocence except for a roguish gleam in one beady watchful eye.

For the rest of the afternoon all talk of kirk affairs was abandoned as the minister sat back comfortably in his chair and allowed himself to be thoroughly entertained by our little feathered friend.

So, all things considered, we had grown to cherish our Wee Comic. With his cage on my knee I carried him about the house to place him in whatever room I happened to be working in at the time. He adored this form of transport and was never bored through having to sit in the one place all day. The hustle and bustle of domestic chores were a positive thrill for him. The sound of running water, the rattle of dishes, the batter of my typewriter, all kept him highly amused, but his most favourite of all was hearing the vacuum cleaner swishing from room to room.

He enjoyed a vast array of foods and would bury his beak into a big, juicy strawberry till his nose and beard were stained red; he could smell oranges a mile away and went daft till a piece was stuck into his cage, no one could eat a bag of potato crisps but he had to have a tiny peck, but his greatest weakness was for mint from any source. If I spoke to him just after I had cleaned my teeth he almost drooled at the mouth as this most delectable of odours washed over him. If I was eating a Polo mint he tried everything he could to get at it and was overjoyed when I tied his very own Polo to the spars of his cage. It lasted him six months and finally broke in the middle from continual scraping and nibbling. He had learned to wet his beak in order to get the fullest possible flavour out of his mint and was most annoyed when Tania, after much careful application of teeth and tongue, managed to extract the broken Polo from the cage and crunch it up in one gullop.

His taste in music was excellent, he showed a distinct preference for light classical, rousing choral renderings, and anything with a Scottish flavour to it, and whenever we had to go out we would leave on one of his favourite tapes to keep him happy, usually one of himself talking interspersed by me talking to him with some music thrown in for the sake of variety.

It was a joke in our house that for such a little guy he owned an awful lot of household effects for we would refer to his table, his records, his tape recorder etc.

Being very aware and proud of his uniqueness it was therefore all the more nerve shattering when one warm, sunny day I nearly lost him. I was sitting outside writing, Tania lolling at my side, Jockey happily ensconced on his hook.

On discovering I had to go indoors to fetch another pen, I tucked my jotters and books about my person and started to propel myself backwards up the ramp which was steep and narrow and difficult to negotiate. So engrossed was I in heaving myself up, using my feet as levers, I forgot all about Jockey hanging behind me and backed full tilt into his cage.

The clips holding the removable bottom section sprang open so that, suddenly, there was nothing but a large gap between Jockey and freedom. The jolt had knocked him off his perch and down he fluttered, so surprised he had no time to do anything to halt his fall and on reaching the sloping cage bottom he rapidly slid towards open air and an uncertain future.

Quick as lightning my hands flashed out to snap the cage shut just as his head reached the aperture and only by a supreme effort on my part did he escape a meeting with Madame Guillotine.

And there I was, sweating and palpitating, perched precariously on the steep ramp, only my slithering feet holding me there in my chair, my jotters and books in a scatter on the ground, Jockey's body half in, half out of the cage, my shaking hands trying not to exert any pressure on the dear little chap's head, every split second that passed making me lose my grip on the ramp. Jockey was making odd, squawking sounds as he tried to extricate himself from the bonds that clamped his neck and with blurring vision I honestly imagined that my green budgie was turning blue.

'KEN!!!' Thank God for the strength of my Glasgow voice box. But Ken did not immediately appear though I bawled his name over and over. Tania couldn't get past my chair to gallop into the house for help so we all three of us remained there, seconds seeming like years, and slowly, slowly my feet were slipping while Jockey's frantic struggles were twisting him into frightening contortions...

Then – Mercy arrived in the shape of my husband, his voice rather annoyed because he had been busily employed in the kitchen plastering the skirtings.

But on spying my predicament his grumbles immediately ceased and between us we soon had Jockey back in his cage and the bottom not only clipped back on but tied round with string for good measure. He remained silent and uncommunicative for fully one hour, during which time he hunched himself into his feathers and eyed my anxious face with beady huffiness.

Then came a belated little chirp, then another, and in a very subdued voice he told himself he was a 'burdie'.

By teatime he was back to his normal self but never again did he hang on his hook under the canopy, instead he simply sat on a little homemade bench beside one or another of us and if we had to leave him for any reason Tania set herself up as his guardian, ever watchful for abandoned cats who wandered the district and who, half wild, would have eaten anything they could get their fangs into, especially a budgie who loved anything that walked on legs, be it two or four, and who would have gone to meet such a fate with open wings and a happy song in his budgie throat.

9

A Tourist Attraction

The bluebells were bursting out everywhere, on the lower slopes of the hills, in among the fresh green grass in the woods where they made a cool, blue, hazy carpet. Clumps of shy primroses burgeoned throughout the mill, while hundreds of other wild flowers starred the banks of road-side ditches. Everything was new and exciting that first summer in the glen. New discoveries were made at every turning and we spent most of our time outside, rain or shine.

There were many who imagined that because we lived so deep in the heart of the country we must hardly see a living soul, but how wrong they were.

People came to see us from all airts and pairts, not just family and friends, but strangers knocking at the door, wanting to know this, that, and the other.

Ours was the first habitation along that stretch of road, so we had tourists regularly stopping to ask directions to the Kyles, Tighnabruaich, Colintraive.

Occasionally an engine boiled over on the steep climb up Mill Brae, and we were called on to supply kettles of water for steaming radiators. Laughingly we told one another that we ought to set ourselves up as a tourist information centre, and charge for our services, as we seemed to be looked upon as some sort of halfway house. One man asked to have his flask filled with hot water, a bolder version wanted his filled with tea, yet another needed help with a punctured bicycle tube, whereupon Ken obligingly helped him fix it and sent him on his way fortified with a cup of tea and several biscuits.

When a short while later I needed patches for a punctured wheelchair tyre, Ken sheepishly admitted that there were none left. He had given the entire repair kit to the cyclist!

Once or twice we were knocked up and asked if we did bed and breakfast and met with most disappointed reactions when such enquiries were answered with a 'no'. Hikers, campers, explorers, and just plain curious passers-by, must have thought we were the 'Keepers of the Mill' as quite a few came to our door to seek our permission to explore the policies.

The American lads from the Polaris submarine base in the Holy Loch were particularly fascinated by the ruins; one young man thought that the mill had been the scene of a battle and eagerly wanted to know all about it. By this time we had acquired some of the history from the villagers, and on several occasions Ken took it upon himself to act as guide and enjoyed himself enormously as he pointed out various features of interest. When he had talked himself hoarse his following went on their way, heads reeling with all the information they had received but feeling very well pleased with themselves, so much so that one lad offered to pay Ken for his time!

People came with their metal detectors to browse amongst the old buildings in the hope of locating artefacts from a bygone age, and it was the funniest thing to watch them skimming their detectors over the ground, looking most serious and intent.

Ornithologists came armed with glasses to watch buzzards and kestrels soaring over the hills, parties of schoolchildren came with their tutors to make notes and generally scramble about. The old iron wagonways over the lades made good, if somewhat narrow, bridges, but, undeterred, people 'tightroped' or 'bummed' it across, according to their gymnastic abilities, their objective being to explore the sturdy remains of gunpowder store buildings and baffle walls situated on the opposite riverbank.

Of course, none of these visitors came all at once. The mill could drowse and dream for days, maybe even weeks, before an 'invasion' interrupted the privacy, and we became so used to thinking of the place as one, big private estate, it always came as something of a shock to us to see people wandering about 'our' fields, and God help them if they dared to pick the daffodils growing inside our garden boundaries.

Later in the season came fishermen who had for years fished the 'Wee Echaig', which, with its deep pots and rushing falls, contained more than many a big river. From Yorkshire, Northumberland and Durham, the fishermen came to ask our permission to park their cars at the wall beside our house. Into the wee sma' hours of morning we could see their lights bobbing about among the trees and the smoke from their fires spiralling upwards, and we hoped it was keeping the midgies at bay. In our part of the world they attacked human flesh with particular ferocity, and were ever present on a calm, damp, summer's evening.

Over the years we became simply Ken and Chris to these

cheery, hardworking men who counted their annual trips to Scotland as the greatest highlight of their lives – despite the midgies!

But the most unexpected visitors of all were the courting couples who arrived late and left much later, and who had the audacity to park their cars right outside our bedroom windows and proceed to kiss and cuddle and do other things that we hoped Evelyn was not observing from her window – even though we couldn't help observing them from ours until we crept guiltily over to shut our curtains.

It was those amorous pairs, not to mention tourists who had the nerve, whenever we were away from the house, to park their vehicles outside our cottage leaving no room for ours when we returned, that prompted Ken to erect a fence around the front of the house into which he set an east and west gate, allowing parking space under the Nothing Room window for our car.

Last but not least, he made up a sign which proudly bore the title 'Powdermill Cottage', and this he fixed to the east gate so that it was the first thing visitors saw as they drove up.

The cottage ran off at a left angle to the road so that there was no danger of passing traffic demolishing our carefully erected fence. Ken then set to and painted the house walls a gleaming white, and forgetting to stop he also painted the massive old gatepillar at the entrance to Stable Lane together with the edging stones we had placed round a little rose garden which we had created in the curving inner wall near the pillar. Meanwhile, I painted the fence and Tania painted herself a whiter shade of pale through leaning against the wet paint as she watched the world go by.

Slitting open old car tyres we turned them inside out to make robust flower tubs, and once they too were painted we placed them round the patio area of the 'west wing'. Inside the fence we made a tiny garden which was soon filled with summer snow, mimulus, tom thumbs, pansies, and a variety of little rock plants.

In nearby Glen Saul, surrounded by craggy blue hills, there was the most beautifully situated tip anyone could wish for, festering and mouldering and smelling quite badly on a warm summer's evening, but the piles of rubbish were kept well covered by the good men who worked there. It was a favourite venue for men looking for spare car parts and for anyone just looking for anything that might prove useful.

We often met friends rooting around the fresh refuse and it was a joke amongst us that only the best people went there. After a good hunt around we found what we wanted, and into Marilla Mini we crammed two abandoned council rubbish containers, the old-fashioned type made of wooden slats held together by circular metal rings.

These we lugged home and into them we inserted plastic buckets with holes punched out of their bottoms. We filled them with earth and rushed off to buy two little conifers. The containers were then placed one on either side of the door, and looked most effective against the snow-white walls.

We convinced ourselves that they didn't look in the least like council litter bins and were most hurt and offended a few days later to find in one an empty coke tin, probably thrown from the school bus window.

But nothing could take away our pride in Polly Powder-mill. We glowed, we swelled with euphoric achievement. We rushed over the road just to stand and stare and hug ourselves with joy, and if a car passed by we pretended to look at anything else except our beautiful little cottage.

We went for short walks along the road so that we could turn and go slowly back to savour the sight of that sparkling white vision set against the green summer hills. It was a wonder, a delight, no one else could possibly have a house like ours, nowhere else could there be such a garden, spilling over as it was with a profusion of white, blue and orange blooms.

Tourist cars and buses slowed down to look, and from behind our bedroom curtains we watched them pointing and nodding and we felt as tall as the mountains surrounding our home.

But what goes up must come down, and after climbing to such dizzy heights we soon came down to earth with, if not a bang, a mighty painful thump. Delightful the cottage might look from outside, but the interior was sorely in need of attention. The bedrooms faced the sunless north and both they and us suffered from rising damp. So Ken rolled up his sleeves and got to work.

The bed was removed from our room and placed in the doubtful privacy of the sitting room. There we slept for several nights, while in daytime Ken lifted up the bedroom floorboards and began the unsavoury task of digging out earth and rubble which went into buckets and thereafter into the deep cavity of a ruin that had once been the boilerhouse, conveniently situated on the perimeter of the west patio.

As is the way of things, when he was deep in the bowels of the bedroom, visitors would arrive and he would emerge, dirty but determinedly courteous, to keep them entertained while I made tea in the kitchen and hoped they wouldn't come through into the sitting room area and see our bed reposing there.

But a few of them were genuinely interested in Polly Powdermill's progress and it wasn't every day they got the opportunity to see a dug-out in the middle of a bedroom floor. Through they would troop to stand on the edge of Ken's excavation and peer into its depths with utmost interest and curiosity, whilst making jolly remarks about digging to Australia and other such joky comments.

'Oh, what ho, old thing, found any gold yet?'

'Gracious! What fun! *Such* an unusual way of passing the time!'

The more down-to-earth ('Do excuse the pun, old thing!') simply said, 'Hell! You'd better watch you don't find any corpses doon there. Never know wi' these old buildings.'

'Help ma boab!' (a famous Glasgow expression) 'the place must be crawlin' wi' creepies! Look at the size o' that spider!'

Whatever they thought or said, or however they said it, they came and looked while they could, for in a matter of days Ken had dug away a good four feet of damp earth, and, having replaced the floorboards and the furniture, we moved back in with the feeling that we were much drier than before, and certainly the musty smell had evaporated.

With the house needing so many improvements we thought it would be a good idea to apply to the local authority for a grant, but first we decided to get estimates from nearby building firms. Up they came, a gleam in their eye on discovering the amount of work needing to be done to bring the house up to 'tolerable standards'.

They must have thought that because I was an author I

must be rolling in money. 'Might as well go the whole hog,' they told us, rhyming it all off – I could almost hear the 'ting' of a till and see the money signs mounting in their eyes.

A new roof; new floors; damp courses; rendering; new windows; a vast amount of plumbing work; a bathroom; new gutters and downpipes; a new septic tank; an improved water-supply system. It went on and on, and when finally we got estimates ranging from £12,000 to £13,000, we sadly put our dreams and notions aside as never, never, could we have found the money to put towards the cost of the work.

Depression settled over us like a black cloak. Visions of piping hot water running through a tap, a beautiful bathroom, slipped away from us like mountain mist, and we told each other gloomily, 'We'll never get Polly Powdermill the way we want it.'

But we soon squared our shoulders, gritted our teeth, and decided firmly we would do it ourselves, bit by bit, over the years.

Ken got to work once more. First of all he removed the bar from the top end of the sitting room. We seldom used it, and it was taking up precious space, so out it came and the room took on a new dimension at once.

The wall that separated the kitchen from the sitting room was composed mainly of plasterboard, with the door opening in near the sink. This caused continual traffic jams not to mention embarrassment, since the opening was directly in line with the living room. Except for a few close friends, our grotty little kitchen was for our eyes only, so the wall was dismantled, board by board, until finally there was nothing separating the sitting room from the kitchen. Of course, the very next day the insurance man came, the fishman popped in, as did the coalman and one or two stray acquaintances, who just 'happened to be passing'.

The tradespeople batted not one eyelid at sight of the scar that was our kitchen, which gaped at them from the far end of the house. No doubt they were used to houses of all sorts, but not so the casual visitors.

'Oh, my, what a big house you have, very open plan!' they exclaimed, and it took me all my time not to add, 'All the better to swallow you up!'

'A bit draughty, though,' came next, so of course we had to grin and bear it and explain what we intended to do with the wall, which was propped up in bits against the book units of the sitting room.

To conventional eyes it must all have seemed rather odd. People did not remove walls and lean them against book-cases, nor did they have the remains of what had once been a built-in bar and its accoutrements littered around the rooms, but we were not the usual run of the mill!

We did things other people didn't, and when everyone had gone we forgot about the inconveniences and had a good laugh about it all.

Within a day or two the wall was back up, and the door was now on the side away from the sink. The relief of washing up without being half-killed by a door thought-lessly flung open was tremendous.

While Ken was in the mood for doing things with walls, he erected another plasterboard section between the kitchen and the Nothing Room so that when it became a 'Something Room', a bathroom we hoped, we would have conformed to the building regulation that stipulated a certain amount of space had to separate the cooking area from the ablutions room. And it was strange that, to enter a little hallway leading nowhere except into the Nothing Room with its small, high window and its piles of odds and sods.

But, like everyone else, Ken had his dreams and longings, and in the course of that year he transferred the bits and pieces from the Nothing Room into the old wash house in the garden and set up some of his model railway so that he could have a place in which to linger and relax whenever he had a spare minute. So the Nothing Room became Powdermill Junction, and the men who disappeared into its portals very quickly became boys and were never seen again until hunger, or the wee sma' hours, or a mixture of both, forced them back to the reality of wives and weans waiting to kiss them home, or clonk them on the head and tell them their dinner was in the oven.

But Ken needed his escape, and when he wasn't tinkering with his engines in Powdermill Junction he was doing things to the house that were not within the bounds of normal imagination.

One of Ken's major endeavours was to jack up the floor of the sitting room to level it out! It sloped so badly I could go to the wall opposite the window, let go of my wheels and whizz backwards at top speed. If the furniture hadn't been propped up with wedges of wood it would have rolled about at crazy angles which would not have been very good for those of our friends who needed perspective in their lives after sampling a good dram or two of the 'water of life'.

With two borrowed car jacks and two of our own, Ken retired under the house and one by one inserted them under the sitting room joists. And of course, when he was thus employed, people came visiting, and what could I do but usher in two friends we hadn't seen in ages?

They immediately spotted the changes in the house. Rushing from the living room to the sitting room they dismally commented that the bar had disappeared into oblivion.

'Oh, and you've also moved the kitchen door,' came the next observation.

'Does everything in this house move around or just disappear?'

At that precise moment everything *was* moving, including themselves, as down below, Ken had started jacking up sections of the floor which, little by little, were moving up accordingly.

Well, If only I'd had a camera sophisticated enough to record the expression on their faces! But we only possessed a little Kodak Brownie, given to me by my sister Kirsty on my twenty-first birthday. It was now fourteen years old and still perfectly capable of taking good outdoor pictures, but was so shabby both Ken and I only sneaked it out when no one else was looking. Wicked devil that I am, I allowed my guests to suffer a few silent, open-mouthed fits before I deigned to tell them what was happening, and then we all grinned in relief, including Ken who had arisen from the bowels, cobwebby but smiling and demanding a cuppy.

He had packed the joist ends with bits of Ballachuillish slate, and when, after tea, he set a spirit level on the floor, he was overjoyed to see the air bubble plunk in the middle.

Our visitors too were impressed, and went off cheerily saying they were glad to get back on terra firma, and proclaiming they couldn't wait to see what else we were getting up to next time they popped in. Through the open door I saw a busload of tourists, all smiling and admiring our wee house, little knowing what went on behind the white walls and the snowy nets that draped the windows.

10

Doctors and Bloodhounds

In the middle of June we installed Gran in the cottage for a fortnight, while Ken, Evelyn and I went off to the island of Mull for a holiday.

There we stayed in a caravan that looked out west to the Treshnish islands, among them the oddly-shaped 'Dutchman's Cap' and famous Staffa, all of them like blue, floating ships on the breast of the ocean.

We were welcomed by fresh eggs and milk and a homely little note that hoped we would enjoy our holiday and that the weather would be kind to us.

Such is the warmth of island hospitality. Margaret, the lady who owned the caravan, was soft-spoken and kindly and popped in every other day to see if we were comfortable.

We had a lovely time on the island. We lazed, we sunbathed, we paddled in the sea with a herd of Highland cows keeping us company, for these great, hairy, gentle beasts like nothing better than to stand in the cool shallows on hot, fly-ridden days.

We drove round to the headland of Ard Dearg to watch huge glorious suns dipping down into the sea with Ulva,

Gometra and Inch Kenneth making striking purple-black etchings against flame-red skies.

I painted little oil sketches of the surrounding scenery; Evelyn made a host of new friends; Ken and I went for long walks in cool gloamings, and we played cards with Neil McColl whose charming cottage with its well-kept garden, was right next door to our van.

We visited Duart Castle, home of the Chief of Clan MacLean, to gaze at its dungeons and look from the windows of the Searoom out over the sparkling blue waters of the Sound of Mull. In the Banqueting Hall we wandered about, looking at lifelike portraits, at family treasures and heirlooms, and then on to an Exhibition of Scouting throughout the Commonwealth.

We met Lord MacLean of Duart who chuckled with delight at the idea of me 'bumming' it up the flights of stairs to gain access to the upper regions of the castle. He told us about the filming of scenes at Duart for Alistair MacLean's film *When Eight Bells Toll*, and of how worried one of the actors had been when his kilt kept billowing about his ears in the helicopter-landing scenes.

We visited beautiful Iona whose turquoise seas had enchanted Queen Victoria, and had the same effect on us as we sighed and gazed and wandered through the mellow ruins of the nunnery where flowers grew on the ancient walls. And we went quiet and respectful to visit the Abbey, where white doves parked themselves decoratively on our hands and shoulders, one sitting on my head for so long I began to fear it had decided to nest there.

On one memorable, breathlessly-hot day we took a trip on a fast launch to Staffa, with Colonel Anderson at the helm and his wife and daughter dispensing tea and delicious home-baking from the tiny galley.

Seals popped their heads out of the blue ocean, watching us with big, intelligent eyes; cormorants stood on the rocks drying their wings and – wonderful sight! – a school of dolphins, complete with babies, leapt and cavorted a short distance from the boat, following us for a good bit of the way as the little craft danced over the waves.

And then Staffa! Oh, breathtaking isle that had inspired Mendelssohn to write his famous 'Fingal's Cave', that immense and awe-inspiring cathedral made up of basaltic lava columns piling into the great dark cavern where the cries of seabirds rang and reverberated. There were other exciting caves, the Clamshell Cave where the columns were curved into the shape of a gigantic shell, and the Boat Cave to the left of the Great Face of Staffa.

Yet Staffa, for all its grandeur, was a mere youngster of around one hundred million years compared to little Iona, which is composed mainly of Lewisian gneiss and is about two thousand, five hundred million years old. I read these figures in a book about Mull and Iona till my head reeled and I was quite unable to take in anything more. In the end I shut the book and just enjoyed what the islands had to offer in the present day and age.

After two weeks of sightseeing and generally lazing about, it was home to Polly Powdermill and to a rapturous welcome from Tania, Jockey, and little Wendy, one of Tania's offspring who now owned Gran, or was it the other way about? We had loved being away but it was even lovelier to be back, and a relief to learn from Gran that everything had gone like clockwork in our absence and that the water hadn't either clogged up or dried up. We had discovered it was liable to do so if the weather was dry for more than a week.

That had come as quite a shock to us, as, when the spring came in and we were just congratulating ourselves that there would be no more freeze-ups, the tap went clonk! clonk! one warm day and refused to yield up one more drop.

The thirsty great trees that clothed the hillsides in drab-green blankets were the culprits. One conifer could suck up gallons of water in a day and there were thousands of them in our glen alone, and more to come, judging by the furrows that we had seen scarring moor and mountain on our travels throughout Argyll.

The older villagers who remembered the 'natural' hills told of a time when the burns had frothed down in abundance and no one had ever gone short of water, no matter the weather.

When our supply had dried up on us we had known for the first time the novelty of going to a deep well in the woods which never ran dry. At least, for me it was a novelty. Ken might have thought differently as he lugged brimming pails along Stable Lane to the house.

But Evelyn never minded. She and I found plenty to occupy us on our way to the well. There were the tadpoles, now rapidly growing legs and looking more frog-like every day, swimming about happily in the old horse-trough outside one of the sheds. Forbye having them in the bath-tub, Evelyn had decided she would like some in the trough, and a good thing too, since the ditches had a habit of drying up in warm weather and the tadpoles were stranded.

The numbers we saved from this fate will never be known, but we were certainly instrumental in keeping up a healthy frog population in the glen.

We also enjoyed watching out for lizards sunning themselves on the old walls of the mill, and of course there were grasshoppers chirruping away in the long grasses and wild flowers to look for; primroses and bluebells and shy little pansies hiding in cool glades.

And I mustn't forget the dragonflies. The first time I saw one of these enormous, gossamer-winged creatures zigzagging about in the air I shouted to Ken, 'Look! A helicopter!'

None of us could ever quite believe the size of these wonderful insects with their golden and black striped bodies and their glorious wings. As they pranced and danced through the air they often came close to us, and one particularly fine specimen actually landed on my knee one day, giving me the chance to observe its wings at close quarters. It was like looking into the iridescent hues of a soap bubble, all shimmering and delicate and trembling in the summer wind.

Evelyn and I were always on the lookout for these and other such fabulous creatures, and Ken would eye us meaningfully as he hurried past and we would pretend to move ourselves a bit faster till he was out of sight. Then we would meander on our way, enjoying the hot sun, the cool green canopies overhead, pointing out the 'candles' on the horse-chestnut trees, Evelyn looking ahead to 'conker time' when we could thread string through the hard red fruits and hold conker competitions.

There was no need to rush about. It wouldn't bring the water back on, and there was so much wonder and delight to be found in the shady woodlands.

In fact, it was the only time we needed to worry about water shortages that summer, for although the days remained warm and sunny they were interspersed with plentiful rain falls, and there were no more trips to the well in the woods.

We were all looking forward to a visit from Mary who had been ill in hospital with a nervous complaint. She was home now and greatly looking forward to a holiday at Polly Powdermill, which she hadn't seen since she had come with me to view it. 'This has been a happy house, Chris, I can feel it all around us,' she had said. Words I had not forgotten and never would. They had come from my darling Mary who had been a mother as well as a sister to us since our Mam had died, and who had always been such a helpmate to us when we most needed her.

But the holiday was a disaster. When she came she wasn't her usual cheery self. She was in great pain from sciatica and had to take to her bed halfway through the first day. For Mary to do that she had to be really ill. She had never had an easy life, it had been beset with one illness after another, but she had seldom complained. Through it all she had smiled, a quiet, warm smile that was oddly sad for often it didn't reach her eyes.

We all hated it when she was ill. She was the one in whom we confided and trusted, and now that Kirsty and Margaret were in far-off Australia she was doubly precious to me and we had grown very close.

Evelyn had willingly given over her bed to her favourite aunt, the novelty of a camp bed in the same room appealing to her adventurous spirit, and of course she loved having Mary's company. All through that weekend they played cards, she read to Mary and carried in her meals on a tray and saw to it that she was never lonely.

But by Sunday evening she was worse and we had to phone our own doctor and go down to the surgery to collect painkillers.

Monday was something of a nightmare and a day I'll never forget. We had to get the doctor in, and while we were waiting for him the SS Bloodhound chose that very morning to pay us his promised visit.

He wanted to know about the financial state of our affairs, and while we were frantically searching out bank statements and other such documents the doctor arrived and marched rather sullenly into Mary's room to examine her. After that, and while Ken was keeping the Bloodhound busy, the doctor motioned me up to the kitchen and told me that Mary would have to go home and be seen by her own doctor. We were to arrange it right away. Having gotten rid of both the doctor and the Bloodhound, Ken rushed up to the phone box to let Mary's husband know she was coming home, and then it was a dash to the ferry; Mary's white face turning just once as she walked away. My heart was sore and sad within me for having to part with her in such a hurried and abrupt manner.

Two days later a letter from the Social Security Department told us there would be no more financial help from them. We had argued that we didn't even have a thousand pounds in the bank and therefore we were entitled to some monetary aid, but to no avail. We were on our own and though the prospect was alarming I was also relieved. I had always felt uneasy in my mind ever since that memorable first visit from the Bloodhound.

Henceforth we drew thirty pounds a week from the bank and, by dint of much careful management, got by on that. Collins/Fontana had bought the paperback rights for

Rhanna, it was coming out in August, things could only get better – and when Ken phoned Mary and found out she was improving things did get better and the world was a brighter place.

I was in the process of incubating another dose of 'flu when the paperback edition of *Rhanna* came out. I had waited and waited for my publisher to send me my 'author's six', which was the agreed amount of complimentary copies due me whenever a new book came out. Every morning, when the postie's van drew up at the door, I held my breath only to let it go in a rasping wheeze when he drove away without delivery of the longed-for parcel.

The first time I glimpsed my paperback was in a window display set up by our local bookshop. Ken rushed over and came back to where I was parked in Marilla Mini. Into my hand he placed my first paperback novel and the thrill of that moment made me forget my blocked nose and my sore throat. I just stared and stared at it in wonder and awe for there is something about a new paperback, especially if it's your own, that is utterly exciting.

The hardback edition of *Rhanna* had of course been my greatest thrill, something that will live with me for all time, but not many people can afford a hardback. They appear briefly in shop windows and afterwards are rarely found on the shelves, except on those of libraries when one book can be read by dozens of people in turn – which is why most first authors have such empty purses.

A paperback was different. If it was successful it would hopefully remain in the public eye for a long time to come and be bought by hundreds. Thousands? Millions? My imagination ran riot, reality flew out of the window. Although *Rhanna* had certainly been popular, I was a long way from being a household name and it would be years before I made the breakthrough. But in those moments I didn't think of that. I was so absorbed in the rapture of the moment I wanted to open my window, wave my paperback about and shout, 'Look! This is mine! I wrote it, I wrote it, I wrote it!'

But of course I didn't. Ken and I just quietly turned the pages eagerly to exclaim and comment, to devour the blurb and tell one another how good his unique little map looked on the endpapers. Then we drove to the hall where our local art club was holding its show, delivered the paintings I had done for the occasion, and drove home where I collapsed into my bed, for once in my life wanting only to get my shivering, sweating flesh under the blankets – and outside the sun was shining fit to bust!

For three days and nights I trembled, sweated, shivered, and never ate a thing. My heart beat so fast I thought it would surely gallop itself to a halt; my sinuses were so blocked I couldn't swallow; my nose dripped like a tap and soon became a swollen red blob in my blotchy face; my lungs heaved for air which only just managed to filter through my choked air passages. Ken danced attendance, Tania tried to get in to see me, but wasn't allowed to because of her ticks, Jockey wolf-whistled from the sitting room but wasn't allowed in either because his piercing whistles rattled my one good eardrum, the other having ruptured when I was a child and was prone to bleeding when I was as full of the cold as I was now.

The only thing that cheered me up was the sight of my paperback and, later, the news that I had sold most of my paintings at the art show.

Then came my six paperbacks, followed by a fifty pound cheque for my paintings, followed by the doctor whom Ken insisted be called in when I was still coughing and gasping after the fourth day.

That was my first meeting with Dr Bill Wilkie who was doing his locum in the absence of our regular doctor. Dr Wilkie was a sandy-haired giant of a man who filled the bedroom when he came striding in to sound my lungs and take my pulse.

I took to him instantly because he was a human being, which not all doctors are. I know this from my hospital experiences as a child. They look at you from a great height, if they look at you at all; they tell you things about your body which you are never meant to understand unless you have swallowed a few medical tomes; their voices are clipped and patronizing and you end up feeling like a wriggling maggot and maybe looking like one too, as you lie there, white, exposed, and ill.

Dr Bill Wilkie was none of these things. He sat on the bed and talked and grinned and looked like a big boy fresh out of school.

After a few minutes of friendly chat I turned the talk to other things. Being an avid Agatha Christie fan I had always fancied writing my own whodunnits, and had in fact penned one whilst residing in the Holy Loch house. It hadn't as yet been sent to a publisher but lay in the wardrobe along with half a dozen or so unfinished manuscripts, but I was keen to gain as much knowledge as I could about crime, and particularly wanted to know about poisons and other such horrors.

Encouraged by my new doctor's friendliness and by the information that he had once done a stint on pathology, I seized my chances and set about asking him to advise me on different methods for bumping people off.

Forgetting about my 'flu miseries I really warmed to my subject, and was so carried away by my own enthusiasm I failed to notice that my listener's attitude had undergone a complete metamorphosis.

Realizing that he was not responding one jot to my rapid questioning, I glanced at him and saw that he had backed away from the bed. His face was noticeably paler than the pink robust countenance that had earlier come through the door, while the eyes behind the glasses were regarding me with wary bewilderment as I came to a croaking halt.

I began to laugh, I chortled and wheezed and shook the bedsprings and only stopped when I could get no more air into my congested lungs.

'Ach, doctor, it's all right,' I hastened to assure, 'I'm a writer – look – on the shelf, there are my books – my novels – my *paperbacks*.'

I placed a good deal of emphasis on the last word. 'Get one,' I instructed, 'and I'll show you.'

He extracted a book, he glanced at the title, at the name, my name, Christine Marion Fraser. He turned the pages, a few minutes later he was convinced that I wasn't some crazy nut with murderous intent in my heart.

We talked, we had a wonderful time, I signed a paperback copy of *Rhanna* for his wife, he wrote out a prescription for me, and he went off beaming like a Cheshire cat.

In the living room an anxious Ken hovered, wondering what had kept the doctor in the sick room for so long.

'Oh, *she'll* live!' laughed the doctor. 'But I'm not so sure about *you*. I think she's planning to bump you off.'

With that he went away leaving Ken to scurry into the bedroom and demand to know 'just what the hell was *that* all about?'

When Mary came back in October she was well and cheery, and I was delighted at the prospect of having her at Polly Powdermill for a whole week.

The days were warm and mellow, the mill a tumble of glorious autumn colours. We talked our heads off about everything under the sun. Mary and I had always been able to have long discussions, yet, looking back, remembering, I realize she never had it in her to indulge in idle gossip about neighbours and friends. Rather, she saw the good in people, even if some of the people we discussed weren't too fussy about the things *they* had to say about others. She was always interested in what we were doing and took a great delight in my books and my writing and had been so proud of me when *Rhanna* was published.

She was also very understanding about the struggles new authors have while trying to make a name for themselves, and about all the hard work that writing entails.

So we sat in the sun and blethered happily; we ambled through the woods, collecting kindling and throwing sticks for Tania who was as delighted as the rest of us to have Mary at the cottage.

We shopped in Dunoon, we visited Younger's Benmore Estate with its beautiful gardens and ornamental ponds, its giant redwood trees, and all around us the rugged hills of Cowal were ablaze with amber and gold and purple.

One day we collected Gran and we all drove to Glen-daruel, Glen of the River of Red Blood, where an angry battle was fought between the Scots and the Norse invaders who were under the command of Meckan, son of Magnus Barefoot, King of Norway.

The Scots won the battle and threw the bodies of their slaughtered enemies into the river which soon ran red with their blood. A huge rock marks the spot where Meckan, the Norse chieftain, is said to be buried with his sword by his side.

I loved to gaze at the river Ruel and to imagine, rather gorily, the noise, the confusion, the fierceness of the battle, but I could never ponder over it for as long as I would like as always something or someone called me back to reality. This time it was Ken, calling me over to where the others were making their way into the little church, with its domed cupola and its atmosphere of history. This was Campbell country and written records told of two Campbell chiefs in the parish who sat in pews on opposite sides of the church because of the feuds and disputes within their own clan. Bloody, exciting days these must have been, and something to wonder at and dwell upon from the comparatively civilized times of the present day.

Coming out of the kirk we wandered about in the quiet little kirkyard with its ancient stones, the river tumbling nearby. Gran, in a pensive mood because she hadn't been too well of late, paused for a moment to absorb the tranquillity, and to say she felt the 'auld man' in her bones and her time would not be long in coming.

And Mary was there beside her, quiet and still and saying nothing, her face sweet and sad, and something in me went sad and silent also, but not for Gran and her spoken thoughts; for life and death and things that went too deep to voice.

The next day Mary and I went to Glen Massan to browse among the bramble bushes, picking berries and not saying very much. And it was good that, to be quiet and peaceful together. We could talk our heads off but we knew instinctively when to be silent and let the peace and the goodness of the countryside wash into our souls.

It was a lovely week, warm, mellow. We saw a red squirrel gathering acorns in the mill, another running along the top of the wall near the cottage, chattering at us for disturbing its browsings. We watched roe deer grazing at the edge of the woods and saw buzzards and kestrels soaring in the wide blue sky – and we looked at the hills and saw that they were no longer green but had faded to shades of ochre and umber.

'The winter will be here soon, Chris,' Mary said on her last day, 'I'll think of you when the hills are covered in snow.'

The next day she went, taking Evelyn with her for a week, and the house was quiet and still – and just a little lonely without Mary's cheery presence.

11

Rat versus Cat

And come the winter did, bringing with it all the old problems of leaks and draughts and mice belting about in the loft looking for shelter and food.

But we had passed the novice stage of living in an old, sadly neglected country cottage. Ken no longer panicked when driving winds blew the rain in under the slates, but calmly climbed aloft to shift his buckets around. Because we had filled in so many cracks and holes and had replaced lengths of skirting, the mice weren't so prolific in the kitchen. Instead, the crafty little beggars found their way into the loft. Reluctantly, Ken set traps which we often heard going off when we were in bed, and we would look at one another. We never said anything beyond expressing the hope that more plaster and more repairs would eliminate the little creatures from the house, as we both hated the idea of those horrible, cruel traps.

As it happened, the mice did eventually vacate the premises that winter, not because of our traps but for a much more sinister reason. At first we didn't notice that the overhead scamperings had become heavier and louder, we just smiled and told one another that the mice must be wearing clogs or that they were growing fat and clumsy from all the pilfered crumbs.

Then one morning I went into the kitchen to a scene of such carnage I honestly thought that some terrible battle had taken place in the night. Surely there must be *a body* lying dead and bloodied in some corner? For there were feathers everywhere, great big yellow and green feathers scattered about the floor, one or two gracefully decorating the table, another caught in the curtains and gently swaying about.

My imagination went wild, ran riot. Jockey! Jockey! My Wee Comic! Yellow and green feathers! Had he somehow in the night attained gigantic proportions, burst out of his cage, only to be savagely molested and slaughtered by some horrific creature that stalked the dark hours, waiting, waiting, to pounce and maim and kill?

But the feathers were huge. And though my bonny budgie was so big and bouncing he had often been referred to as a parrot, he certainly wasn't *that* big! I gulped, I flew to the living room to whip off Jockey's cover and found him hale and hearty and blinking at me in some annoyance for having uncovered him with such unseemly haste.

Relief sighed out of me. The others were up, crowding into the kitchen to gape and comment and wonder, and finally to gather up the feathers and place them in the bin and thereafter to have a post mortem over the breakfast table. Try as we might, none of us could come up with a solution to the strange *Mystery of the Feathers*.

Two days later the answer to that and one or two other mysteries was resolved when I opened the bottom drawer of a little kitchen cabinet. Here all the household cleaning materials were kept, here had I kept the brightly coloured feather duster which enjoyed a pretty easy life as not one member of the Polly Powdermill clan was overly fond of housework. All that remained of the duster was one sorry bedraggled green feather attached precariously to a mish-mash of wood that had once been a fairly stout length of cane. Opening the drawer wider I saw the toothmarks, or rather the gnawed remains of the drawer-back, which was over an inch thick and made of pretty tough wood to boot.

'A wee mouse couldn't have done that,' I said to Ken in some trepidation.

'A rat!' He sounded very positive. 'That explains the noises in the loft, not mice, but a bloody great rat with fangs on it like Dracula!'

I stared, I imagined; the dark, silent kitchen, the slinking rat, ferociously chewing its way into the drawer hoping to find food and finding instead polish and brushes and dust-ers. I pictured its frustration, taking it out on the feather duster, pulling it through the gnawed aperture, leaving behind the torn-off cane, attacking the rest in the middle of our kitchen in a frenzy of rage.

Mice we could endure but not rats, certainly not in the house. The very idea of it under the same roof as us sent the shivers along our spines.

Ken waged all-out war on Rat. 'It might be breeding in the loft for all we know,' he said grimly, and very courageously went up in the loft to look. But there was no sign of a nest, and Rat never appeared in the daytime. We always just heard it at night, thundering about overhead, scratching and scampering. Occasionally we heard a high-pitched screaming sound that raised the hairs on my neck, but we didn't know if Rat was just screeching for the sake of it or if he had attacked and murdered a little mouse who

115

had been foolish enough to venture aloft.

Tania had by this time got scent of it. She had grown rather blasé where the mice were concerned, and quite frequently went sound asleep when she was supposed to be on Mouse Duty, but the odour of Rat did things to her placid nature. Her hackles would rise along with her muzzle, low growls would issue from her throat, and Mouse Duty was forgotten with this new and exciting discovery.

And then we saw Rat. One evening we were all ensconced peacefully by the fire when Tania, who had been fast asleep and dreaming judging by her twitching paws and whiskers, suddenly leapt to her feet and went bounding into the kitchen, low growls rumbling deep in her throat.

In seconds all hell seemed to be let loose within the kitchen premises. Tania had never been too graceful on her feet, more like an elephant than a ballet dancer, and we heard the crashing of furniture, the sound of scrabbling paws followed by high-pitched excited barks – and then silence. With one accord we left the fire and rushed up to the kitchen, expecting to find – what? A great black rat attached to our darling dog's jugular? A huge white dog attached to the jugular of a big black rat? Silence hit us, a silence charged with venom and hatred and fear so thick you could taste it.

Ken righted a chair, Evelyn scooped the contents of the waste bin back into place and set it out of the way.

Tania was over by the cooker, sprawled her full length, her panting tongue hanging so far out it had made a little damp circle on the lino, her ears were pricked forward, every hair, every whisker bristled with utmost intensity. She looked up as we approached and wagged her tail as if to say, 'It's all right, I've cornered the brute, he won't get away now.'

And she had. We peered cautiously into the dark space behind the cooker. Two malevolent glinting eyes stared back at us and I held my breath. Most of God's creatures I love, some I tolerate, others repel me, but no matter what I never fail to feel fascinated, be it a large, slimy black slug, a blood-engorged tick – or an enormous black rat with round pink ears, a long, twitching nose, and a tail so long it disappeared among the cobwebs and dust behind the cooker.

For Rat was big – King Rat – he deserved that title if nothing else. Evelyn had rushed to fetch her torch and shine it upon him, which made him cringe backwards and flatten his ears and show his glistening teeth in a none too friendly gesture.

Tania was growing impatient, she wanted to do things with Rat and to hell with all the gaping and the awe and the wild remarks flying about. She wanted fur, not words, to fly through the air. After all, she had got Rat in a corner, it was her privilege to go in for the kill.

But before she could move, Ken raced away into the bedroom and came back carrying the powerful air gun I had given him for his birthday some years before. Evelyn and I looked at one another and with one accord erupted into screeches of laughter.

But Ken wasn't laughing. He was incensed, bloodlust shone in his eyes, and before we could gather our breath and our wits he had taken a pot shot at Rat.

The reaction was immediate and furious. Rat stood up on his hind legs, a sound in his throat started off as a chitter of rage and rose in crescendo till it became a high eerie scream of fear and fury.

Ken's shot had gone wild, Rat had not been hurt but he

was fighting for everything he held dear: life, freedom, safety.

The inevitable happened. I began to feel sorry for the poor, trapped creature. It was really rather pitiful, three large human beings, one large hairy white dog, all ganging up on a poor little rat who had never really done any of us any harm.

I voiced my thoughts, so too did Evelyn whose compassion for Rat had been born along with mine.

'Harmless?' frothed Ken. 'Defenceless? These brutes carry disease of every sort. He'll have to go – this very night!'

He did. While we were fighting and bickering Rat saw his opportunity and slunk away, to where I don't know. Neither, it seemed, did Tania, who let out a yelp of frustration and spent the remainder of the evening with her nose questing into every crack and crevice the kitchen had to offer. But to no avail, Rat had gone, for the time being, and meanwhile Ken made a decision.

'Rat poison,' he decided firmly. 'I'll get that bugger somehow.'

But rat poison wasn't so easy to come by, in fact it seemed a near impossibility to get it at all though we scoured every possible and impossible shop we could find.

In desperation Ken sought the help of our neighbour who lived in what had been the mill manager's house across the road. Rick was Yorkshire born and bred, he had contacts for everything and seemed to know everyone that it was useful to know.

'Leave it to me,' he told Ken. 'We'll get the booger between us. I've a score to settle with that rat myself.'

It transpired that he too had been visited by Rat, despite

the fact that he owned a large feline creature called Cat (no one had been able to think up a fancier title when he had arrived as a tiny kitten). Cat was big and black and sleek, and he stalked the night hours like some slinking black panther in search of prey. He caught mice by the dozen and laid them at Rick's door in neat little rows, but so far his efforts to catch Rat had all been in vain.

In due course an innocent-looking brown bag came into Ken's hands. The bag contained a quantity of blue grains and these Ken mixed with porridge oats. He then placed the saucer in the loft.

Well, saucer after saucer of blue porridge oats disappeared regularly and still we heard noises in the loft like a football team at injury time. Ken doubled the dose of rat poison but to no avail. Rat's footsteps were, if anything, even louder than before, and when we glimpsed him over by the old changing sheds he looked bigger and sleeker than ever with no indication of having devoured anything more potent than Pears toilet soap.

I had imagined him lying bleeding and helpless in some dark, godless corner, dying slowly and painfully, and my heart had gone out to him, but not so. Rat was made of stern stuff, he was pitting his wits against ours – and he was winning.

'The brute's indestructible,' moaned Ken. 'Before we know it he'll have a wife and weans and we'll be overrun by dirty, stinking black rats.'

By this time the rat poison was finished and the mouse trap big enough to catch a creature of Rat's size hadn't been made.

Life went on, of course, and Rat went on, plundering, stealing, performing his lone nightly clog dances on the rafters. No other member of his species was heard, sighted, or scented; he was enjoying himself, using his cunning to survive, allowing Tania only enough scentings and glimpsings to drive her crazy, but no more than that. Never again did he appear in the kitchen before we were abed, yet he managed to sneak there in the middle of the night and devour soap and plaster and anything else he could get his fangs into, all under Tania's nose, for she had opted to sleep in the kitchen ever since Rat's spectacular battle with the feather duster.

Then one night there was silence. No rustling, scampering, squeaking, screaming or chittering. No bits of plaster falling, no teeth jarring, nor sound of gnawing, no scraping of wood, nothing. The silence was so deep it was uncanny, and for quite a long time neither Ken nor I could get to sleep for straining our ears upwards, listening – listening for the sounds that never came.

The next morning we found Rat stretched out by the east door: huge, black, sinewy – and dead. There was no mark upon him, he looked peacefully asleep, as if he had been arranged to look that way. There was no horror now, only one four-legged creature with long whiskers, a pink nose, and thick, oily fur. I felt pity, I felt shame, he had fought, he had survived, he had lost, he had died.

He had been a clever old Rat, but not as clever or as strong as Cat who had stalked the night and who had won. He had murdered Rat, he was content.

Cat was over there, over by the old ruin in the middle of the field, washing his face, pausing for a moment to look towards the cottage and us, something about his expression making me feel creepy, and sad for Rat lying still and dead in the morning sun.

120

Cat was smug, too smug. A few weeks later he was killed by a car on the road and kicked carelessly into the ditch. We all felt sorry. He had been a lovely cat and a marvellous mouser – and he had proven that he could also kill rats. But he hadn't been smart enough to avoid death on the road and we lifted him from his watery grave and gave him a proper burial as befitted a cat as beautiful and as clever as he.

We never saw another rat again, only the water rats down by the riverbanks and they never came near the house. So Rat and Cat met their end, and in their own different ways they were special and part of the mosaic that was the life we lived at Polly Powdermill.

12

A Gay Day

As our second winter in the glen progressed we soon realized that Rat had been the least of our problems. On stormy nights, draughts whistled through the living and sitting rooms at top speed and we hugged the fire and worried that Jockey might catch cold, even though he remained on top of the world and was busily practising his forthcoming Christmas speech to the nation! At least, that was what we told visitors. What he was trying to say, and finally mastered with the utmost enthusiasm, was: 'Oh, it's a gay day...' A pause, then triumphantly, 'It's a wee gay day the day!'

Influenced by Larry Grayson on the telly (yes, we had finally succumbed to 'the box', though only viewing in small doses), I had gone round the house, belting out the well-known expression in my own inimitable fashion, little dreaming that one small person would pick it up.

But I should have known better. Jockey was a budgie who had dedicated his life to listening to my voice and repeating the things that took his fancy, usually those that we did not want to be repeated for ears other than our own.

So 'gay day' reverberated through the house along with

the winter gales. In desperation we hung curtains over the aperture that separated the two living areas. They flapped merrily in the breezes and looked terrible. When one of our friends popped behind the curtains and asked that 'Father Ken' hear her confession, we suspected that our draught excluders were not quite the latest thing in home decor; when another, and much quieter, acquaintance couldn't resist winding the curtains round his face to say, 'And now, kiddies, for my next trick...' our suspicions were confirmed.

That very night I took my mail order catalogue to bed and both Ken and I delved into its pages. After much debate we sent off for a pair of folding doors with frosted-glass panels and as soon as they arrived they were promptly fixed in position.

As well as looking good they soon proved most effective as draught excluders and it was bliss to confine the heat of the fire to the living room instead of having it dilute itself on its way through the house.

The paraffin heater kept the sitting room cosy, so at least our living quarters were much more comfortable, and Jockey was so pleased with himself his gay days came out fast and furious followed by raspberries so rich and thick you could almost taste the colour of them.

Electric convector heaters in the kitchen and bedrooms took away the chill, but as the ever-hungry meter in the porch gulped up fifty pence coins as if they were going out of fashion, we only burned the heaters at mealtimes and bedtimes.

By now I had started work on the third Rhanna book and was growing dissatisfied with my cold, cramped window ledge.

The advent of the TV had effectively curtailed the length of my writing day. Evelyn naturally enjoyed watching her favourite programmes and I had perforce to stop work around five o'clock when family affairs got underway. There being no other room in the house suitable enough for me to continue my writing in, I was forced into the boredom of watching TV. But I could never have wasted my precious time simply goggling at the box, and kept my hands so busy with knitting I soon had made an Aran trouser suit for myself and jumpers for Evelyn and Ken.

Ken and I discussed the problem, and just before Christmas we hit on the idea of a caravan. 'I could convert it to suit,' Ken told me, his blue eyes shining. 'There's plenty of space down by the old wash house at the east corner of the garden.'

The more we talked the more enthusiastic we grew. We perused the 'For Sale' columns of the local paper, looking for a van of the right size and – just as important – the right price!

At last we spotted one and rushed down to Glen Massan to see it, all keen and panting, and praying that no one else had gotten there before us. We didn't stop to think that not many people would be looking for a caravan in the middle of winter and we were most anxious to be first on the scene.

We were, of course! There was no army of would-be purchasers waiting to greet us. In fact, there was no one, not even the caravan owner, yet in many ways we were glad of that fact. It gave us the chance to look the van over without someone breathing down our necks, and it also gave us the chance to explore that most perfect place, the 'Golden Gates' entrance to Benmore Estate, all pine trees and pine cones and mossy earth covered in russet needles.

124

The Golden Gates were quite famous. Bus parties came to look at them, artists painted them, I myself had done a little watercolour sketch, depicting the gates and the trees and the mountains beyond.

The gates were exquisitely fashioned in wrought iron which had been painted a golden-bronze colour. On the other side of them was a most picturesque lodge house and – beside it – my caravan. In my mind it was already mine. I couldn't bear it if someone else got it now, not after we had gone through the gates and had examined the outside of it. We drooled, we exclaimed. It was just what we wanted, broad enough to accommodate a writer's accoutrements, plenty of space inside for a wheelchair to get around – for of course we had peered in the windows and thoroughly snooped around. Nor was it too expensive either. It was, in fact, just perfect and parked as it was in such an exquisite setting it was an easy enough matter for me to visualize myself in there, writing my books, cosy, alone – and private!

The dream came true: we met the owner, money was handed over, the transaction was complete. The interior of the van was all we had hoped for and I was in such a haze of delight I went round the house in a euphoric cloud. I voiced my joy, over and over. 'It's a gay day!' I yelled the minute I opened my eyes each morning. My poor, long-suffering husband groaned aloud in his despair, through the wall Evelyn moaned and groaned also, while, from the sitting room, unbelievably one morning, a little sleepy voice echoed my words, still under his night wrappings but ready to greet the day with his current favourite expression.

Bedtime also brought out the daftness in me. Quite often I had what Ken called my 'mad half hour' when I would talk such a load of nonsense we both ended up sore with laughing and fell asleep, exhausted. With the prospect of my caravan looming on the horizon I was madder than ever, but I soon came down to earth when we discussed the problem of getting the caravan safely home.

And it was a problem. It had been in the one spot for so long it had dug itself comfortably in; one of the tyres was perished and useless and wouldn't have supported a wheelchair, let alone a heavy caravan. We rushed around looking for a suitable wheel, in between Christmas shopping, mice safaris, tree felling (into the woods once more to chop down our tree), business affairs, and all the hundred and one things that seem to pile up as the festive season approaches.

At last we found a wheel of the proper dimensions; our local garage promised to tow the van to its new home, and we settled down to await the great day.

I say 'settled', but for my part I seethed with impatience. While we waited, Ken and I haunted the area of the Golden Gates. We held the key to the van and in we went to plan all sorts of things, especially the creation of a door broad enough to allow my wheelchair through. The existing door was so narrow I had to get down on hands and knees to crawl inside, but such inconveniences were of small import in those breathless days of excitement. Enough it was that I was the proud owner of a caravan that was mine! mine! mine! My passport to peace and privacy.

'I wonder how many books will be written in this,' Ken pondered as I poked around, but I was too much in the clouds to give a thought to actually working in my latest acquisition. I was looking ahead to spring days when I could go down to my den and make tea on the neat little stove, and perhaps even sleep the night on one of the couch beds over by the big picture window.

The day came, Jimmy arrived with his young son. A sprinkling of fresh snow lay on the ground, the hills of Glen Massan were remote and beautiful.

The rusty old nuts on the dud wheel had to be sawn off but that didn't take long. Soon the new wheel was fitted and the van was hitched to the back of Jimmy's Land Rover. Off we went, Ken and I following in Marilla Mini as a back-up system in case anything went wrong.

But nothing did go wrong, at least not on the journey to Polly Powdermill. We all chanted along at about 15 m.p.h. holding up the traffic on the short stretch of main road that had to be traversed before the turning for the glen.

After that it was plain sailing to Mill Brae where the Land Rover puffed and panted as it hauled the van up the slippery hill.

Then it was the 'breest o' the brae' and the cottage, big grins and sighs and Ken rushing out to guide Jimmy through the gates into Stable Lane. The woodland path was mushy with dead leaves and much manoeuvring had to be done to get the van round a tight corner where a grassy slope led down to the river.

Then, catastrophe! The van slithered, pulling the Land Rover sideways, Ken shouted, the engines revved, the exhaust poured smoke, one of the van's rear wheels sunk groaning into a deep culvert that was always filled with water, but was now an underground torrent after weeks of rain and melting snow.

Planks of wood were sought, found, carried to the disaster scene and into the house I went to worry and fume but remain rational enough to make tea, a good hot cuppy being the Scotswoman's answer to every problem under the sun.

An hour later, oh glorious sight! My yellow and white caravan sailing along the river path at the foot of the field. Rushing to the east door I watched it being positioned into place, across from the old wash house, its big picture window looking towards the fields and the trees and the river and the snuggle of wintry ochre hills in the distance.

In that perfect setting many books were to be written, dozens of paintings created, countless dreams dreamt and plans made, but for now I thought only of the men and their struggles to bring my caravan home.

Into the house they trooped to drink tea and eat cakes and warm themselves by the fire. They soon thawed and looked none the worse for their adventure, they talked and laughed and I talked and laughed with them, calm seeming, not at all interested in anything that lay beyond the chatter and the fire and the cheery analysis of the day's escapades.

When they had gone Ken and I looked at one another, without another word he seized my chair to rush me outside and somehow manhandle me down the steep, rough slope to the caravan.

It was freezing cold but we went in to open the curtains so that we could look at the view I would see as I sat writing my books and painting my pictures.

The door faced out on to open country and we opened it so that we could better see the trees and the hills and the mill ruins dreaming so peacefully in the pale winter fields. Down below, the river gushed and foamed, the wind soughed through the woodlands.

Half frozen and with drips at our noses, we looked and listened, and Ken raced up to the house to bring down steaming mugs of tea so that we could linger till it was almost dark and we could see no more. But before the last vestiges of light departed the sky, Evelyn came home on the bus and she too came to drink tea and poke into drawers and cupboards, while Tania, who always had to be where we were, sniffed around the corners, tail a-wagging but after a while wondering what all the fuss was about – as she so plainly conveyed with a short sharp 'woof' and a glance over her departing shoulder when it had become so dark outside we could hardly see one another inside.

In the days that followed Ken battened down the van against the winter gales, he wired it up to a switch in the porch, and hey presto! there was light! He buried a length of hose in the ground, connected one end to an outside tap, the other to that in the van, and there was water – just as long as it didn't freeze up, clog up, or dry up!

One of the single berths was removed to make way for a little desk that he had made from bits of an old desk and a discarded set of drawers. Ken loved wood, he loved the smell of it, the feel of it, he loved working with it and never threw any away if he could help it.

The result was my little desk, neat but practical with three good-sized drawers on one side, unexpected shelves for books and jotters and so on, and plenty of knee room for my wheelchair.

I loved it! I adored it! My boxes of paints, my brushes, my canvases, were brought down from the house and arranged in the wardrobe within easy reach. Down came my typewriter, my jotters, paper – oodles of that – all the books I needed for research. Between us we arranged them all into place, except for the books which lay about in piles – but not for long! The hammer and saw were busy for a day or two until a bookcase took shape and was brought into its new home, to be filled immediately with a large selection of publications.

A fan heater was plugged in under the desk, and bliss! Warmth flooded my den, curled round my toes, around my heart too. I was in seventh heaven and felt that nothing could ever surpass those days of joyous achievement. No one else in the world had a little den like mine, snug and safe, with windows that looked out on to the wild, sweet hills, and a door that opened on to quiet lands where the deer listened and watched beneath the trees, and God walked down from the mists that veiled the shadowed corries. Nor had anyone a dear little robin like mine, a robin who came and stood on the gatepost outside my window to chatter at me until I opened the door and threw him some of the oats I kept in a jar especially for him.

The advent of Christmas made us abandon work on the van and then it was Christmas trees and holly, logs spluttering in the grate, country walks in frost and snow, mild rains blowing in from the west, the magic of Christmas Eve when it was so good to come back to our little house sitting snug and tranquil under the stars.

And then Hogmanay carrying us into January 1980, all quiet and calm after the rush and excitement of the festive season.

I hadn't managed to get down to my den for some time. The steep slope leading to it had been slippery with ice and was really very unsuitable for a wheelchair. But Ken was soon busy, laying earth and rubble ramps, making shuttered concrete retaining walls to keep everything in place. He had made some money doing freelance artwork, and promptly spent the lot getting a local builder to come and lay concrete on the arrangement of zigzagging paths and ramps. The Social Work Department erected handrails on either side of the lower and most difficult ramp. They also employed Archie the Blacksmith to fix up a most ingenious pulley affair with weights attached, the idea being that I should hook up my wheelchair on the way down in case I broke the speed limit, not to mention my head! It was also intended that I should hook myself up whilst ascending, thus taking the weight off my arms and feet, and we all smiled and nodded and agreed that the pulley was a wonderful invention.

Meantime, Ken cut an aperture in the side of the van facing on to the path and into this opening he fitted a new, much broader door which allowed my wheelchair straight through.

For a time everything went smoothly, everything worked well, though me being the impatient, unconventional creature I had always been, I chose to ignore the help of the pulley on the way down and simply whizzed along to my den, using my hands and feet as brakes. On upward journeys I obediently hooked myself up and slithered sideways like a crab, since I was only able to attach one side of my chair to the formidable hook.

Even then I only ever got half way up, and, hanging precariously on to the rail with one hand, I had to ungrapple myself with the other, turn myself round and ascend the next part backwards, pushing with my hands and feet. A short rest at the foot of the next ramp, pant! puff! then on, ever upwards, no handrails to assist; another rest then on to the next ramp, and finally, the short, steep slope up to the door where the Wee Comic had almost met his end.

In all, there were four summits to negotiate (to *me* they felt like summits), and in the end I only attempted to go up on my own if I couldn't attract assistance from the house.

Eventually the pulley broke away from the wall, much to my relief. Thrift and gratitude had been instilled in me from the cradle and I had felt obliged to use the pulley in order to justify its existence. Now it was no more, and I was glad when Ken put it away in the shed just in case it might come in useful for something.

After that we got into a routine. Every day after lunch I went down to work in my den, Ken faithfully bringing me a mug of tea at three o'clock as I was often so engrossed in what I was doing I would never have remembered to make tea on my own little stove.

At five o'clock every night Evelyn appeared to help me up to the house. If I was terribly busy and anxious to get on, I went back down after tea, but, with winter dark all around and perhaps squalls of rain and wind battering on the roof, it was too lonely and cut off even for me and I had to force myself to abandon the brightness and life of the house for the deep, still, solitude of my den.

However, I needed no coaxing to go down in the kindly light of day, taking my time about it, pausing every minute to gaze at the hills, to look for signs of life in the rockeries Ken had made on either side of the handrail, to peer with joy at the daffodil spikes poking through the grass at the edge of the path.

In my pocket I always carried some crumbs for Robbie who was there every day on his fence post. He had become so tame he would flutter down to my feet to peck away at his crumbs, his breast feathers ruffling in the wind, his little head cocked, looking up at me with bright, trusting eyes. Then, real joy! Unexpected, unanticipated. Early afternoon. A pale January sun peeping above the shoulder of Fraser's Hill, brushing the frosty fields with gold, burnishing the dead bracken, kissing the bowed heads of the snowdrops, breathing life into the gaunt, grey stones of the mill ruins... and Robbie, fluttering to greet me, tic, tic-ing a happy welcome, not waiting for the crumbs to be strewn but instead coming to perch on the arm of my chair, little stick-like legs straight and sure, spidery feet splayed out, eyes bright, watchful, friendly.

And me, hardly daring to breathe, muscles rigid, murmuring daft-like, saying the things I might say to Jockey, Robbie listening, engrossed in the nonsense, in the 'pretty Robbies' and the soft whistles.

Unforgettable moments. Just a wee robin and me, alone in the gold of the winter sun, sharing the wildness and the sweetness of sleeping bens, understanding the voice of the rushing river, the lonely sighing of the wind in the trees.

He was my Robbie, my secret, my delight each day as he perched on my chair and ate my crumbs and stood on his post outside my window, watching me working, scolding me for not being out there with him, waiting for three o'clock and the tea and the man footsteps to die away before he was down and standing outside the field door to receive his meal of porridge oats.

But it didn't last. Such magic never does. Towards the end of January he was there as usual, waiting patiently on his post as I came down the ramp. He came, he perched on my chair, he chattered, I spoke. Then he hopped down, I threw him his crumbs and he fed for a while before carrying away a piece of bread to the haven of the little Christmas tree we had left in the garden till it could be sawn up for the fire. Robbie felt safe under its branches. Indeed all the wild birds sheltered under it when the icy winds blew and the chill rains fell.

I sat and watched Robbie under the tree. A shadow came down from the sky, swiftly, silently. The bare branches of the little tree offered scant protection as the great buzzard swooped and struck and plucked Robbie from the ground.

In front of my eyes, the magnificent buzzard, the tiny robin. He looked so safe and snug cradled in those great talons, riding on that last, cruel journey. Even as I watched, his dear little head drooped on to his red breast and I knew he saw nothing more of the day or of the sun shining pale and golden above the hills.

The buzzard rose, glided swiftly away and soon he was a shadow again, black against the blue of the sky.

Beneath the branches of the tree was a scatter of glossy brown feathers and the little piece of bread I had given Robbie that he might survive the winter.

13

The Yellow Peril

January 1980 had seen the publication of *Rhanna at War*, followed in May of that same year with *Blue Above the Chimneys*. For the latter it was back to the Albany Hotel in Glasgow where I underwent two days of television, radio and newspaper interviews, before Bob Cowan whisked Ken and me through to Edinburgh. There I was steered round the bookshops to meet the booksellers and was utterly taken aback when I was presented with a large bouquet of flowers from the staff of The Edinburgh Bookshop. I stuttered out my thanks and said that the kind gesture had made me feel famous.

'But you *are* famous,' I was told. 'We all love your books and feel that we know you so well from reading your auto-biography.'

Whereupon for the first time I wondered if I had done the right thing in exposing so much of my life to strangers. But it was too late to turn back now, and there was nothing else I could do but grin and bear it and somehow keep myself detached from it all.

Despite my apprehensions I was thrilled beyond words by all the glamour and excitement, but nothing could ever match the thrill I had experienced a couple of months earlier when I had become the delighted owner of a butter-coloured, battery-driven buggy, with a top speed of four m.p.h., three on hills, two on Mill Brae.

I had never imagined I would get a chance to drive one of these jolly little Batricars, let alone own one, but Ken had persuaded me to buy it, trotting out so many reasonable arguments that I had finally and rather fearfully succumbed.

We had, at that time, just over one thousand pounds in the bank, an incredible sum of money for a couple who had never had two spare pennies to rub together. Most of the savings had accrued from sales of our paintings which were becoming much in demand in the area and had also sold well at local art shows.

Any book royalties that had come in had immediately gone out again in payment of things for the house, but the money for our artistic efforts went into savings to go towards a new roof, a bathroom, a thousand and one things the cottage so badly needed to make it a complete home.

But Ken's mind was on the more immediate future. He had sent away for literature that displayed beautiful, gleaming buggies – the Batricar being the one he liked best.

Rather sourly I had gone through the brochures with him but always I came up with the same old argument, 'We can't afford it.' But secretly I sneaked out the brochure to look, and pine, over the tempting illustrations of little buggies all in a row, all in different, bright colours.

Oh, to know the freedom such a vehicle would bring into my life. I had spent too many years using a manually-propelled wheelchair with Ken puffing away at the helm as he pushed me up hill and down dale.

We argued, we discussed, we talked ourselves blue in the

face, and in the end I allowed Ken to win simply because my own resolves were rapidly weakening under such pressure.

All we had ever done since leaving our rented farm cottage, our first home, was scrimp and scrape and put our all into one set of walls after another. There had been the suburban bungalow, the Holy Loch house, and now Polly Powdermill, all old properties, all needing drastic renovation and decoration, all a drain on finances that had never been particularly bountiful. We had had few holidays in our lives, and had never been able to afford anything more luxurious than tents and caravans.

Ken pointed out that I had worked long and hard and had never really bought anything to make being disabled any easier. We could go on and on fixing up old houses till we were old and grey and in the end unfit to drive anything more complex than a lawnmower.

Well, that did it! The idea of becoming feeble and old without knowing real freedom was just too much for me to bear. I was young, I told myself firmly, I needed to grow and expand and have new experiences and I needed to do it now while I was eager for everything that life had to offer.

We arranged to have a demonstration on a Batricar and from the minute I sat in that darling little machine I was hooked and didn't know how I was going to contain myself till my very own Batricar arrived.

The day finally dawned and I fairly bubbled over with exaltation inside. I had never been one to readily display my feelings, except perhaps to close members of my own family. But Ken knew how I felt, so too did Evelyn, who for a child of her age showed remarkable restraint from the minute she first clapped eyes on my buggy which I had immediately christened the Yellow Peril, not really knowing what that meant till Ken put me straight, but by then it was too late.

The Yellow Peril was here to stay and none of us could wait to get out and examine it in detail. Never once did Evelyn try to tinker with it or drive it as any other child of her age might have done. Ken had already explained to her that it was not a toy but a hard-won mode of independence for her mother, who had waited a long time to buy the dear little buggy sitting at the front door, all yellow and gleaming.

And then the longed-for moment came, the thrill, the wonder, of getting into the Yellow Peril and driving away on my own, away down the road towards Mill Brae, which had always been too difficult for Ken to attempt simply because he could never have pushed me back up that formidable incline.

When out in my chair, gathering kindling or just merely out for a wander, I had only ever been able to sit on the 'breest o' the brae' and gaze longingly down on forbidden fruits, but now! All that was done with and I fairly scudded towards the brae, laughing, tossing all my former restraints to the wind now that I was alone and there was no one to witness the daft, eager, carefree self I so often kept locked inside.

I think I went a little mad. I laughed aloud with sheer abandon and throwing back my head I yelled *'Freedom'* over and over, till the echoes reverberated in the woodlands and rose triumphantly to the surrounding hills.

On down to Rumbling Bridge I went, named so because of the tremendous boom and roar made by the river as it gushed down from the glen. It is said that the Romans built the ancient, moss-bound bridge. Whether that is true or not, it was a tremendous place to be after heavy rain or melting snow had sent the hill burns tumbling into the Wee Echaig, and the rushing brown river thundered its way along to the sea.

A new bridge had taken the road away from 'The Rumbler' so that one could sit in peace under canopies of oak and watch the water steaming over numerous falls and gurgle into dozens of potholes etched into the rocks. Yet it was from the new bridge that the best sound effects were to be had, as I discovered one day when I had paused for reflection.

But all that was in the future. Enough it was for me to have reached the bridge under my own steam, as it were, and I sat and savoured the untamed splendour of a Scottish river in full, tumultuous spate.

I had never minded my own company, in fact there were times when I positively had to have it in order to think and ponder and get my own particular world into perspective.

But on that momentous day, when true *freedom* became mine, after spending twenty-odd years of my life in the confines of a wheelchair, ten minutes of my own thoughts were quite adequate and I couldn't get back up the hill fast enough in order to relate my experiences to Ken.

To an able bod that might seem odd, to count a simple journey down a steep hill as one of life's unforgettable adventures, but for me that first lone journey in Yellow Peril was one I'll never forget all the days of my life, no matter what other excitements lie on my horizon.

Ken listened, his eyes shining while I babbled on, conveying to him my delight in my little buggy and the pleasure of having taken the plunge and bought it. He never said, 'I told you so'; instead he smiled and got into Yellow Peril to drive it down an earth ramp he had made at the back of the house. This led to the old cow shed, where a space had been cleared in readiness for the great day and a power point had been fixed up in order to charge the two powerful batteries that gave life to the little machine.

After that I became a familiar sight in Yellow Peril with my faithful Tania at my side. She had batted not one white eyelash the first time I had taken her for a walk down Mill Brae in my new mode of transport, rather she took to the whole thing with great enthusiasm and could never hear the whine of the wheels but she was out like a shot, waiting with wagging tail for me to take her wherever I would.

I grew to know Brig O'Doon very well and liked nothing better than to stop and blether with the villagers on my way into the heartlands of the glen.

The buggy also brought freedom to Ken. I knew I had never been a burden to him; we propped one another up in our own different ways and helped each other all we could.

For one thing, I was the only driver in the family. Ken was nervous behind a wheel so it was my responsibility to get us all from A to B.

Since the days of my first invalid car I had taken to driving like a duck to water but I have yet to meet someone who didn't immediately assume that Ken, as the able bod of the team, must be the one who drove the family car.

I was also aware that there were a few people who, without actually saying as much, truly believed that Ken must be a chap in a million to have taken on the responsibility of a disabled wife. Of course he was a chap in a million, a lot of women must think that of their husbands, but he was far from being a saint and had married me for what I was, and the years had proved that I was far from being a burden to him or anyone else.

Some things were beyond me, though. I have to swallow my pride and admit that. I had relied on him to haul me about in my chair and had always been keenly aware of the physical effort involved. Even though I was a thoroughbred of around eight stones, and proud of it, I had sometimes wished I weighed a bit less for his sake.

Now there was Yellow Peril and his days of hiking along at my back were over. We could go along side by side, no more struggles, no more cares. Whole new vistas opened up for us – treks along forestry roads took us into the hills till it seemed we could touch the sky even while the world lay at our feet; walks through the mill where at last I could touch the old stones and seek out wild flowers growing in places that had previously been inaccessible.

Holidays, too, took on a whole new dimension. We invested in a little trailer, fitted a tow bar to Marilla Mini, and towed the Yellow Peril to the Highlands and Islands. Rough paths, beaches, tracks, trails, fields, hills, the buggy took them all in its stride.

So jolly and happy was the little machine people waved from cars, buses, lorries, smiling, smiling, all the while. Children were fascinated by it and Ken always had an audience when he was loading and unloading it. Quite a few able bods looked at it with envy and said it would be just the thing to get them around the countryside. There was nothing disabled looking about it and I wallowed in the fact that, for the first time since long-ago childhood, I was as good and as whole as anyone else in the big wide world.

Tania had never had so many outings and was fitter than

she had ever been, while Ken joked that he had grown three inches shorter from all the exercise. I retaliated by telling him to get up off his knees and hurry up – or get left behind – for even though the buggy was supposed to go at walking pace it was faster than any able bod on two good feet.

For once I had the upper hand of those out-of-date souls who had smiled down upon me and had told me how nice it was that I could get out for walkies in my wheelchair, and how good it was for me to breathe in the good fresh air, though 'mind you don't catch cold, dear', all smiles and nods and muffled to their old eyeballs in layers of fur.

14

A Smashing Time!

All things considered, 1980 was a good year for us. Not long after the advent of the Yellow Peril, we got a new Marilla Mini. It was a government issue car, as was its predecessor, and it would be ours till Evelyn was sixteen, though with mobility allowance looming on the horizon we hoped we could perhaps have a vehicle of our own choice one day as the government cars were always Minis except for special cases.

Not being a special case our cars had been Minis, but we had always had a soft spot for them even though a wheelchair, a large dog, a growing child and two adults crowded inside it were a perpetually tight squeeze.

New Marilla was pageant blue and it had that lovely fresh aroma about it that made you worry about every grain of dirt, every muddy footprint that found its way on to the unmarked carpets, the pristine upholstery.

But Tania's big, hairy paws, the wheels of my chair, Evelyn's scruffy wellingtons, Ken's wet shoes, soon changed all that and new Marilla settled in and became one of the family.

Our second summer at Polly Powdermill saw us just as busy as the first.

One one side of the wall Jockey sat on his bench, belting out his increasingly amusing repertoire. He always loved rolling his 'r's and lately he had gone to town on one particular word so that 'Jockey's a cheeky wee buggerrrrrr' came out fast and furious. When he got tired of that it was just 'buggerrrrr', followed by deliciously rich and utterly rude raspberries.

'Ay, you're in fine tongue the day, Ken,' the postman said when he stopped to deliver the mail.

'Oh, it isn't me it's...' He stopped with a grin.

'Ay, I know who it is,' laughed the postman and went on his way.

On the other side of the wall from Jockey I was painting the fence while Ken was giving the house a fresh coat of white exterior emulsion.

A request had been sent to Ken's brother in Glasgow, and that very day John arrived, his car piled high with louvre doors of varying sizes.

'For cupboards?' asked Doreen cautiously. She was well used to our madcap ideas and didn't even raise one questioning eyebrow when the answer came back.

'Windows,' Ken was beaming from ear to ear. 'The doors are for shutters – yellow shutters.'

'Yellow shutters,' Doreen confirmed his words. She eyed the house, all sparkling white except for the stonework round the windows which was black.

'SNP colours,' nodded John.

'Ay, right enough,' Ken sounded surprised but both his brother and his sister-in-law knew him well and just laughed.

'Yellow should look good against the white,' was Doreen's verdict.

144

It did. Not just good but beautiful, distinctive, unique – at least to us.

In a matter of days we had painted the shutters and Ken then fixed them up on the walls on either side of the windows. He climbed up on the roof and liberally coated the chimney pots with the same paint, a deep marigold-yellow. A band of black paint was added to the tops of the pots. The result?

'An enchanted cottage!' That verdict came from an artist friend who was eyeing the house as if she would like to paint it too – on canvas.

The next opinion came from a Glasgow couple.

'Och, look is that no' smashin'. It's like thon wee fairy hoose in Hansel and Gretel – zat no' right, Jimmy?'

Jimmy received a strong poke in the ribs. He had been thoughtfully sizing up the mill policies. 'Ay, smashin', Betty,' he was moved to agree. 'It's a rare place a' thegither. You could have a still doon in the woods there and nobody would know.'

The cottage did indeed look 'smashin'. We put so much of ourselves into it, love, sweat, tears – quite often tears because we were still no nearer to getting a bathroom or a hot water supply. Nevertheless we were proud of our home though rather disconcerted when tourist buses stopped to stare at 'the author's cottage', the couriers having now included us in their itinerary of tourist attractions.

And then it wasn't just the house, it was *me*.

Trundling happily along in Yellow Peril, Tania at my side, I did not at first realize that the buses weren't slowing down out of consideration as they passed my little machine.

Then it dawned. The drivers were slowing down to allow the passengers a good long gape at myself!

For some time after that my forays into the big wide world were furtive and embarrassed. When touring buses came along I turned my head away, hoping that I looked as ordinary and inconspicuous as anyone else – in a bright yellow buggy with a snowy white dog at my wheels!

Tania didn't mind. In fact she positively revelled in the notoriety. She smiled at cars as they passed by, tooting and waving, and after a while I smiled too. At sight of a bus I braced myself and faced my public with cheery grins and waves and went on my way, feeling uplifted by all the happy faces that had acknowledged me from vehicle windows.

As the summer drew to a close I was inside that same 'smashin' wee house, literally smashing down walls with a pickaxe. One Sunday morning I got up, had breakfast, went through to the porch with nothing more purposeful in my mind than opening the door for a breath of fresh air.

It had been raining in the night, pouring in fact, water had gushed in under the front door, the porch was swimming. Everything looked dismal and grey and old, the smell of mouldy damp was very strong.

Ken had left the axe propped up beside the brush. Automatically I reached for the latter in order to slosh the rainwater out of the east door – but something in me made me pick up the axe instead and I went to work, not wildly, but calmly and purposefully.

We had discussed the possibility of knocking down the outer porch wall and of replacing it with a big picture window and glass doors but then the summer had come and we had been caught up in the happy joys of that season.

But summer was over now – and it was raining, and I had

146

quite simply had enough of swimming porches and musty smells to last me a lifetime.

By the time Ken and Evelyn were up and crowding in to see what was happening, I had demolished a rotten old wooden cupboard under the tiny windows and was starting on the actual stonework.

Ken didn't rant or rave or shout. No one did.

'I suppose it had to be started sometime,' was all he said, a trifle dourly to be sure, 'but you might have waited for a dry day.'

'Ach, what better way to pass a wet Sunday,' I returned breathlessly and went on with my task.

Evelyn's eyes were gleaming. She spat on her hands, rubbed them together, seized the pickaxe from me and wielded a mighty blow at the bricks. Perhaps there is something in all of us that enjoys a spot of demolition – just as long as such drastic activities are confined to one's own property with improvement in mind.

And if ever anything needed improving it was that porch. It had been an addition to the cottage, the door leading into the living room had been the original outer door through which east winds must have whistled at top speed. They still whistled, perhaps not with the same vigour, but come in they did via the ill-fitting windows and doors.

The poor old porch had outlived its usefulness so we all rolled up our sleeves and set to with a will. By late afternoon the windows had been removed and most of the outer walls demolished, though of course Ken first took the precaution of jamming supporting struts of wood under the roof. The worst of the east winds wouldn't come till January, which was fortunate for us as we only remembered that fact *after* the wall had been removed. All that remained now was the half wall that divided the main part of the porch from the jawbox enclosure together with the dark oblong of the side door, still intact in its frame.

'Best leave it in case of draughts,' Ken decided seriously, seemingly quite oblivious to the fact that there was nothing between us and the outside world but a yawning gap which made the door obsolete.

Evelyn giggled, we all giggled, Tania thought it was wonderful not to have to wait at the door to get out but could come and go as she pleased.

But only for a short while. Before night came down Ken had covered the hole with sheets of polythene that slapped about in the breeze but at least it kept out most of the rain.

An order for window frames went to a firm across the water. A Dunoon glazier jotted down our glass requirements – mostly safety glass – and we settled back to wait – and wait – and wait.

September came in, the frames arrived but still we waited for the glass.

'We should never have pulled down that wall,' Ken mourned. 'We should have held back and done everything the proper way.'

He should have known by now that I never did things the 'proper' way.

'We would have waited forever,' I replied, unrepentantly. 'Don't worry, we'll get the glass before the winter comes. And think how lovely it will be to look out on the snow through a big picture window.'

There was still no sign of the glass when I was laid up with another hefty dose of 'flu that forced me to take to my bed once more.

148

'It's the draughts from that porch,' Ken told me severely. 'That's what's done it.'

'It isn't the draughts, it's the Germans!' I wheezed but he didn't laugh and went stomping away to take his frustrations out on the porch where work was forging ahead despite the lack of glass.

I was still wallowing in bed, feeling like one of those big wet drips you see in the TV adverts for Askit powders, when Mary came for a week. Because I couldn't collect her she arrived at the cottage in a taxi and minutes later she popped her head round my door, all smiles and pleased to be back.

'Don't come in,' I gasped, 'you'll get the 'flu.'

'Och, I've had it,' was her cheery reply, 'I've had everything.'

Without more ado she plonked herself down on the bed and proceeded to give me all her news. We talked and talked, one thing leading to another till soon we were reminiscing about our Govan days. I loved it when Mary started talking about her girlhood as, since she was so much older than me, thirteen years to be exact, she could tell me things I would otherwise have known nothing about. It was fun hearing her talk about my other half-sister and two half-brothers who had been grown up when I was born. Mary spoke of when they were all children together and all the things they did. But times had been even harder for them than they were when I was a child, and even if they had wanted to stay on at school to further their education the financial difficulties in an ever-increasing family would have made it impossible. Mary had become a breadwinner in her early teens but she spoke cheerily of her days working

149

in a factory, though by the time she was nineteen or twenty she was married and starting a family of her own.

I loved it best when she spoke about my maternal grandmother who had died before I was born. I had always wanted a grandmother and from Mary's descriptions of Grannie Margaret I was able to visualize a rosy-cheeked, snowy-haired old lady with an Aberdonian accent whose pockets never failed to yield up a black strippit mint humbug and who dipped her fingers in the sugar bowl when no one was looking.

Grannie Margaret was also extremely fond of snuff and Mary well remembered being sent 'roond tae the shoppie on the corner' to buy 'a wee droppie of snuff for Grannie'. She used to watch in fascination as the old lady 'snuffed and sneezed and wheezed' and when she was done with all that she sat herself back in her chair and declared, 'My, that was grand, lassie, but mind now, no' a word to the old goat ben the room,' the old goat being my own father who had not approved much of Grannie's ways.

It was lovely hearing about the 'olden days'. I forgot my 'flu miseries, Mary forgot all about unpacking, she hadn't even stopped to remove her coat.

Not until Ken came in to say that lunch was ready did we remember that such a thing as time existed and with one accord stared in amazement at the clock.

She was the tonic I needed. That night I got up, the next day I felt so much better I got dressed and we went for a walk.

It was her first glimpse of Yellow Peril. 'Oh, Chris,' she cried, 'I'm so glad you got it, you deserve it so much, I just wish you could have had something like it years ago. It would have made your life so much easier.'

We were able to go further afield than we had ever been before.

It was a golden autumn, I remember it so well, the red and yellow rowans on the hill; the leaves of the alders, looking for all the world like big, golden, round pennies, the slightest hint of a breeze making them dance and tremble when no other leaf or blade of grass moved. One almost expected them to tinkle out a little tune as they fluttered, fairy-like, on their branches.

The heather was at its best, acres of it misting the moors with purple, huge clumps of it growing all along the wayside. The harebells were out too, peeping shyly out of the long, bleached grasses, such delicate flowers both in colour and form, blending harmoniously with great trails of purple clover into which the bumble bees delved in busy frenzy.

At Rumbling Bridge the salmon were coming up from the sea. It was a wonderful experience to watch their silvery bodies arching up out of the creamy brown pools as valiantly they leapt the falls time and again in their efforts to reach their breeding grounds.

Mary was in good spirits, she enjoyed her stay to the full, she didn't mind the mess in the porch, or rather, what had once been the porch. She didn't mind any of the inconveniences, but then, she never had; she took it all in her stride and made no complaint.

Yet for all her cheery chatter there was a weariness about her that had never been there before. She was the same Mary she had always been, easy-going, pleasant, eager to join in our outings, but she was always glad to get back home and sink into a chair with her eyes closed, as if she had been tired all along but hadn't wanted to keep us back.

151

'The porch will be finished next time I come,' she said brightly as she was leaving, 'there's always something different every time.'

'You'll see it when you come in the spring, Mary.' I was sad suddenly at the thought of not seeing her again till many months had passed.

'I'm looking forward to it already,' she returned and went quickly out to the car.

A few days later our glass arrived and Ken was able to fit it into the waiting frames. He had made a fine job of rebuilding the old place. What had been a dismal entrance was now bright and airy with a new window in the cludge, another where the old east door had been and a huge picture window looking out over the fields.

The floor had been raised so that it was on the same level as the rest of the cottage and I no longer had that annoying step to negotiate on my way in and out of the living room. We now had a vestibule with a glass east door leading out to a much more gradual ramp, and all in all everyone was pleased with the transformation.

It was a 'real' entrance, with carpets and soft lights, paintings on the panel plank walls; an electric convector heater that enabled my cherished plants to live in comfort, instead of being half-frozen as previously. Finally, a curtain rail was fitted all round the windows and inner door areas so that in the evenings we could pull heavy drapes right round and keep the house really snug.

What a difference it all made. Ken was well pleased with himself, we were well pleased with him.

That was our cosiest winter to date but it was not without

its escapades.

Ken thought that he would like a caravan too, to be used as an office-cum-model railway layout.

We found one going cheap and got one of the farmers to tow it in on his tractor. It arrived in snow and got stuck in the same culvert that had claimed mine. As it was being pulled out, the farmer discovered a puncture in one of his enormous tractor wheels.

An SOS went out. In due course a second tractor arrived to pull out the first – never mind the poor old caravan groaning on its lopsided axles. That caravan was never meant to be, I see that now. The second tractor also developed a puncture and everyone went home in disgruntled silence.

The next day a third tractor arrived, pulling a trailer in which one huge wheel reposed in amongst dung and hay.

The first tractor got the wheel, the second one had to wait. In the fullness of time a lorry arrived with another wheel, an army of men descended.

The snowbound landscape looked like a battlefield with vehicles littered about and men marching purposefully everywhere.

'We can't pay them all!' I wailed to Ken while I rummaged frantically in my purse. 'It was only supposed to be one farmer!'

For a time it seemed that the second tractor *and* the lorry were fated to being bogged down in the snow, but after much hauling and straining both vehicles jolted clear of the icy culvert and a great cheer went up. In the end everything was mended, the caravan was pulled out of its watery hole and towed into place under the back windows of Polly Powdermill. The first farmer got paid, the others got a dram and were allowed a visit to Powdermill Junction, good humour was restored and everyone went home.

Ken went to work on his van, pulling out all the fixtures to make way for his railway, creating a neat little office at one partitioned-off end.

It was a mistake to remove the fixtures, even allowing for the fact that he propped up the seams with bits of wood. Come the really heavy snows of winter the roof collapsed under the weight of its icy quilt.

One night we went to bed and the caravan was there under the windows, solid and whole, the next morning it had disappeared under an avalanche of snow, only the little office part remaining firm and unmoved.

'Well, at least I hadn't moved in any of my railway stuff,' said Ken with philosophical dignity. 'And at least I wasn't inside the damned thing when it caved in.'

Both Evelyn and myself were profusely sympathetic.

'And at least,' Evelyn concluded thoughtfully, 'it can't spring any leaks now – you have that to be thankful for.'

Ken and I eyed one another. It was one way of looking at it, an entirely fresh angle bearing in mind what was now an age-old problem.

My own caravan was leaking like a sieve so that I had to wind my way round bowls and buckets. The dog, the loft, the cowshed, I had joined the ranks.

We looked at one another in silence for quite a few moments, then we all burst out laughing and went to make a snowman.

15

Back to the Green Hills

In the early spring of 1981 a letter arrived for me. Ken and I had been 'out the messages' and had just got home. I was in the process of getting myself out of Marilla Mini and on to my chair. Ken had gone to open the door and came back to me waving a letter.

At sight of it my heart leapt. We were both in a sort of frenzy at that time, always waiting to see what the postie had brought.

Things weren't going too well with my books. Towards the end of 1979 my friendly little publishers, Blond & Briggs, had been bought over by another publishing firm. This happened all the time in the publishing world, though when I had teetered on the brink of my writing career I had been as ignorant of that as I had been of so much else, and even now, more than two years after the publication of *Rhanna*, I was still very much in the dark about everything.

It was hard being a Scottish writer writing about Scotland. You were in a backwater, far removed from the London scene and all that went on there.

You were a lone soul, typing away in some solitary corner, striving to make your name and your voice heard while you wondered if there was anyone out there looking or listening.

In my opinion it's doubly hard to become a successful writer if your birthplace happens to be Scotland. You have to struggle to prove yourself, to try and tell those half-deaf southern ears that your books are loved by all who read them if great sheafs of fan mail were anything to go by. You have to try and instil into them that the English public do understand what you have written and want more, much more of the same.

But the prejudice is there, and you must try harder. You have to prove over and over that you have not got heather growing out your ears, but are living in a fairly sophisticated country, a country renowned throughout history for its famous sons and daughters.

The book world is a mercenary one. A publisher can hype a book and turn it into a blockbusting bestseller by spending a lot of money promoting it and pushing it into the public eye. Or they can allow a title into the bookshops and let the public find out for themselves if it's worth reading or not.

I came into the last category. Word of mouth, recommendation, the enthusiasm of the Scottish booksellers for my work; gradually, gradually the gospel was spreading around the country – but not very widely in England. Yet English readers were my most enthusiastic fans and were not slow to write in praise. Many had bought my books while holidaying in Scotland – and what a wonderful discovery! Why couldn't they find them in England?

Why not indeed? Simply because I had never been shouted about from the rooftops, and because the bigger English booksellers were unwilling to put me, a Scottish novelist, on their shelves.

156

But there were others who were on my side, beavering away on my behalf, selling my books into the bookshops, slowly getting my name known. The reps – the good, hardworking boys who believed in my books and did their damndest to sell them.

There were others, my champions, every one. I didn't know them yet but one day I would and be grateful to them for everything they ever did for me.

As it was, it was now 1981 and I had still to meet someone from that big busy world of London publishing. My stints in Glasgow and Edinburgh had been unattended in that respect, and now that Blond & Briggs had been all but swallowed up my chances of meeting even an editor were growing dimmer and more distant.

My B & B editor had been warm and friendly and helpful but I had known her for less than two years and had never met her. Now here I was, landed with a new and strange publisher who didn't appear in the least interested in me or my books, and who hadn't even bothered to get me an editor. I wasn't a big name, I wasn't important. They didn't encourage new talent as Blond & Briggs had done.

To cap it all, Collins/Fontana, who had so willingly published *Rhanna* in paperback, were digging in their heels over *Rhanna at War*. For a long time there was silence from them. Ken was never away from the phone box in the village, trying to goad my new publishers into some sort of action, but they just hummed and hawed and passed the buck to someone else and that someone else promised to chase up Collins/Fontana but never seemed to be very successful.

When finally we managed to extract some sort of response it was to the effect that the book didn't please

Fontana in its present form and they wanted it revised.

Since the revision stipulated that one of the characters I had allowed to die in the B & B hardcover edition must be resurrected and allowed to live on, I too dug in my heels.

The book would smack of a Hammer horror film, I declared, with people rising from mist-bound graves to walk bloody nights and haunt their relatives forevermore.

Stalemate existed for quite some time over that one. My Scottish pride surged strong in my veins – but in the end I realized that it wasn't going to get me anywhere. I was a very new writer, I needed all the breaks I could get. No one was queuing at my door begging me to sign sheafs of contracts. I was out on a limb, I was worried, apprehensive – and scared.

So I capitulated. In the depths of the previous winter, afternoon and night, I had gone to my lonely caravan to rewrite great hunks of *Rhanna at War*, tearing bits out and tearing out chunks of my heart with them for they had been good, those bits. I *knew* they were good, people had written to tell me so, but I was in no position to argue with editors and so I remoulded my baby, tore it apart limb by limb and tacked it all together again.

I well remember sitting there, the cold and dark all around, the lights of the house shining like friendly beacons in the black night. I felt alone, unloved by editors and publishers, and the world in general. I was probably suffering from a bad dose of self-pity and as that was the one condition I thoroughly disliked in anyone else I made sure I gave no hint of my feelings to another living soul.

I wallowed alone, lost in bitter thoughts, quite often just sitting there staring into space instead of getting on with my laborious task.

For there is nothing worse than going back to a book you have already written. The feeling is akin to going back to a painting you have created and been well pleased with. You remember every loving brushstroke, striving to get certain details just right, then, having said to yourself, 'Well that's it, finished,' you then go completely mad and daub out your beautiful lochs and hills and collapse in a heap all over the ruined canvas and drown yourself in a flood of tears.

Only in the case of *Rhanna at War* I had not gone mad, someone else had and I didn't like them very well. I spent quite a lot of my precious time disliking the person thoroughly, then when I was finished with that, not to mention a good few swearing sessions, I felt much better and was able to get on with my work.

The typewriter buzzed, the bits and pieces were taken away and – greatest irony – I added in chapters I had written into my original manuscript but which Blond & Briggs had wanted taken out before *they* would publish. I was flummoxed, frustrated, fatigued. I would never understand publishers, they would never understand me. Scottish, oh so Scottish, me with my pride and my reserve and my lack of experience of their sophisticated world that seemed to me then to be full of bloody-minded editors.

But I am glad that the Fontana editor stuck to her loaded guns. She was right and I was wrong. I see that now and I admit it freely.

Never thinking I would go on writing the Rhanna books I had killed off Babbie, the young district nurse who had come to the island to assist 'Auld Biddy'.

In the revised version of the book, Babbie was resurrected and allowed to live a full and happy life. It was a better ending altogether as love and romance were able to flourish for born-again Babbie.

I couldn't foresee the difficulties I was creating for myself in raising the young nurse from the dead. Bookworms are a very astute breed. Those that had read the hardback version of *Rhanna at War* and had perhaps wept over Babbie's demise, would later, in the third Rhanna, find her very much alive and kicking and making her presence felt on the island.

And of course such bookworms would be utterly mystified by the whole affair and would set their own pens to paper to hint gently that I had suffered some kind of mental blackout between one book and the next and couldn't quite remember which character was meant to be alive or dead!

But all that was in the future. Enough it was for the moment that I had sent off my revised manuscript and was, in that early spring of 1981, waiting to hear my paperback editor's verdict.

I ached, longed, pined for the postie to bring me a letter bearing the familiar London stamp and when Ken came out of the cottage waving a letter my heart leapt.

But there was no exciting London stamp on this one, and the writing was unfamiliar. Nevertheless it *was* a letter and being too impatient to wait till I got inside I tore it open there and then.

It was from Mary's eldest daughter Catherine, telling me that her mother was terminally ill with stomach cancer. She had undergone major surgery but there was no knowing if she would survive the operation. The letter went on to say more but I was too shocked to read on.

Enclosed was a note and though it bore Mary's words it hadn't been written by her.

Dear Chris, forgive me for not writing sooner but I haven't been too well, the trouble is with my stomach. Catherine is writing this for me. I've to go into hospital tonight for an operation and after that I should be all right.

It seems such a long time since last autumn but when this is over with I hope I'll see you again. I trust you are well yourself, hen, don't work too hard...'

I could read no further. The world spun, whirled away. I couldn't believe any of it, not there in that sunlit world with the birds singing from every tree and the daffodils dancing in the breezes.

At first it didn't really register. Her letter had only briefly referred to herself, she had quickly gone on to me. 'I hope you are well yourself, I hope you are well...'

The words drummed in my brain. Mary had always hoped people were well even when she herself might be ill. But though she had never enjoyed really good health, I had never imagined that anything could go seriously wrong with her. All the family had turned to Mary for advice and comfort; always patient and wise, she had listened to our problems and had helped in whatever way she could. I had taken it as a matter of course that I would have her for a long time in my life. It had never entered my head that she would die – not Mary – the darling sister who had been like a mother to us when Mam died...

Ken saw my face, he took the letter and read it.

'Oh, God,' he murmured, 'it isn't real.'

It wasn't real, nothing was real. I felt too numb to think straight. When Ken went rushing up to the village phone box I sat in the cottage, unable to move, waiting, waiting – for what?

He came back. Mary had come through the operation, she was holding her own, that was all.

The icy bubble burst inside my heart. I cried and couldn't stop – and to this day I never have, not inside myself where the rawest of wounds never heal in the recesses of the human soul.

Evelyn cried too when she heard the news. 'I wanted to show her my birthday things,' she sobbed.

'You will,' I promised. She was only a child. The most important thing to her in these moments was that her adored aunt should see the things she had recently received for her eleventh birthday.

The next day Ken and I travelled by car, boat, train, taxi, to the Western Infirmary in Glasgow. The journey was something of a nightmare. We never seemed to get there. When we got to the hospital we never seemed to reach Mary. So many corridors, so many lifts – but at last – Mary! Unbelievably, sitting up in bed and drinking a glass of milk. She saw us, her face lit, broke into smiles. How could she look like that? Smile like that? After all she had been through. She was a fighter, that was why. She hugged us, kissed us, so enthralled to see us she spilt some of her milk over the counterpane. Strange how little details like that stick in the mind.

She was trembling a bit, I remember that also. She was surrounded, almost engulfed by cards and flowers, from neighbours, friends, family, from the minister to whose church she belonged and for which she gave so much willing time and help.

'I never knew people liked me so much, Chris,' she said wonderingly. She meant it. She had always underestimated her value to others.

Some of the flowers had been wired from Australia. I could well imagine the agony of Kirsty and Margaret. So far away, so helpless. They wouldn't be able to take it in, it had all been so sudden, they wouldn't believe it, they would have to know more...

They had phoned the hospital, Mary was full of the phone call. 'From Australia, Chris, Kirsty and Margaret. I must have been quite ill to make them do that.'

Quite ill. I looked at her. Hope surged in my breast. She had been through major surgery, it had been touch and go, but here she was, alive, smiling – pale to be sure – but no thinner, still rounded and smooth of limb.

She wasn't going to die, the operation had been a success, Mary was going to live. I convinced myself of that as I sat in that bright hospital room looking at Mary surrounded by cards and flowers.

Thank God for Ken! He was able to talk, the small talk that was so essential in traumatic minutes like these. I felt suddenly weak, with reaction? With relief? With sadness? I don't know. There were questions I wanted to ask, questions I should ask, but a strange kind of caution made me hold back. I remembered Catherine's letter – terminally ill – I had to watch what I said.

I had never held back from asking Mary anything. It was the beginning, the start of long, weary months of deception and soul-searching.

'It was an obstruction, Chris,' Mary volunteered the answer to my unspoken question. She had been in agony, she told us, the doctors wouldn't operate, not until she was

163

almost at the end of her endurance...

'I've never seen my mother cry before,' Catherine had written in her letter. 'She must have been in dreadful pain to make her do that...'

'They've given me a colostomy, look, Chris,' she pulled back the blankets, my blood froze, tears sprang to my eyes, I bit them back, she mustn't see... She did. 'Don't worry, Chris,' she said lightly. 'It was a bit of a shock to waken and discover it but the nurses are marvellous. They show me what to do, I'll learn to live with it. At least I'm alive, I have that to be thankful for.'

We talked, buoyantly on Mary's part. She was full of optimism, delighted that her ordeal was over.

Pray God that it is, I thought to myself. She can't have come through all this for it to be in vain, it would be too much to bear.

'I'll be back to Polly Powdermill,' she vowed as we were leaving. 'Back to the green hills.'

We said goodbye and turned to go. The woman in the next bed was in a post-operative daze, Mary was talking to her, her warm, sweet voice came clearly, 'You'll be fine in the morning, it takes a wee while. I had my op three days ago and I'm raring to go already.'

She turned her face towards us, she was smiling and waving. Her brave words were ringing in my head... 'I'll learn to live with it...'

My heart swelled with grief and pain. If anybody could live with such a thing, Mary could. She had learned to put up with many trials in her life but her greatest trial was yet to come.

*

'It's a gay day!' Jockey yelled the minute we brought him and Tania home from Gran's. Outside the sun was shining, the promise of summer lay over the burgeoning country-side, primroses were peeping, lambs were gambolling, the birds were singing their courtship songs from every bush and tree.

But for me it was a grey day, the world had never seemed so bleak since Mam had died, taking the sunshine from all our lives. It had come back of course, that sunshine, that love for the beauty of life and for the people who make it the sweet thing it is. But always there's a small quiet corner of the heart where the sunshine and the laughter are dimmed forever and I was very aware of its bleakness in the long, uncertain days that lay ahead of me that year.

16

The Time Has Come

Mary was allowed home surprisingly soon. As often as we could, Ken and I travelled to Glasgow to see her. Each time we saw a change in her, she grew thinner, smaller somehow, but she never ceased to believe that she was getting better.

'The doctor said it would take time, Chris,' she would say, and then I would catch a look in her eyes, a strange look that contradicted her optimistic words and I knew that she was waiting for me to reassure her – to tell her yes, it would take time but that in the end her patience would pay off.

All my life I had been interested in medicine. As a child I had devoured an old medical book of Mam's, skipping over the 'dirty' bits that so enthralled my brothers and sisters, poring over instead the descriptions of illnesses and cures. My years in hospital had strengthened my interest. I hated being a patient but badly wanted to become a doctor, and I had gone home to immerse myself in all the medical books I could get my hands on. I started to keep what I grandly (but privately) called my Medical Journal. Inside its stiff, navy blue covers, facts and observations were neatly jotted down. I drew anatomical diagrams of the human body, really intricate stuff, all the organs and bones carefully tagged, the function of each one paragraphed beneath the various sections.

When I realized my disability would never allow me to become a doctor, a nurse either for that matter, I did not cast aside my books amidst a flood of melodramatic weeping. I kept on being interested and, to this day, whenever TV quiz programmes involve medical questions, ten to one I get them right though I might fail dismally in all else.

Doctors have regarded me with annoyance, amusement, downright rudeness, whenever I have dared to hold forth an opinion about the workings of my own body. They are probably quite right to feel as they do. They are the experts, they are used to their patients doing as they are told.

Nevertheless, I feel it is my right to question, to probe, to ask why I have to take this and that drug, and what the effects will be on my innards. I had enjoyed discussing these things with Mary, like me she had an enquiring mind. She was a great reader, she had never been ashamed of her body, she was frank, open and honest about herself. She had shown me how her colostomy worked, her poor thin hands shaking a bit because it was sore, oh so raw and painful a thing to live with, but she gritted her teeth and got on with it and never once said, 'Why me?'

If she had indeed been getting better, if she had been growing rosier and plumper and enjoying life, it would all have been worth it, but she wasn't doing any of these things, she was fading before our eyes, growing weaker, more fragile, a ghost of everything she had been before.

And more and more she turned to me for reassurance, not fearfully but quietly and gently and in a way that suggested she knew I was going to tell her the things she needed to hear.

The honesty that had grown between us over the years withered and died like a summer flower. I lied, I deceived, I said things that sounded truthful and good and which made Mary happy for a little while even while I died inside myself with sorrow.

To manage to eat a simple meal was, for her, a small triumph. From the phone box in the glen Ken and I talked to her, we shared her ups and downs, her pleasure and her pain, dread in our bellies whenever we picked up the phone, relief in our hearts when we put it down again having heard her voice, that easy, pleasant voice we knew and loved so well.

In July we went off once more to the same caravan on the island of Mull. It poured, dismally, coldly, every day. We spoke to Mary from a phone box beside a river with cows licking the glass panes and me in my chair half in, half out of the box, expecting at any minute to feel a big wet bovine nose slobbering down my neck.

Cows are very curious creatures. They stare at you from under their long lashes, they blow down their noses and roll their eyes and bellow at you, showing large portions of green tongue and worn-down teeth. If the mood takes them, and it usually does when they are being particularly anxious to show off or mark their territory, I can never quite be sure which, they stand in a row, sunny side up, lift their tails into a sort of question mark, and urinate and defecate in alarming quantities.

Only when they are satisfied that every last drop has

departed do they lower their tails, though the odd one or two might remain suspended, as if their owners aren't exactly sure what to do with them next. The show over, they lick one another with clumsy affection, eyes a-rolling, ears a-flicking, then, taking their time about it they amble off into the sunset in udder-swinging splendour, leaving you staring at mini oceans of steaming dung, wildly wondering how you're going to wade your way through – wheels and all.

This happened almost every evening while we were phoning Mary. It became *The Saga of Dunghills*, and how Mary laughed as she listened to our descriptions of those 'steamy nights'.

Of course I embroidered each episode with all the might of my imagination. It was so good to hear that laugh, and far away as she was, only a voice on the line, with the misted hills all around and the sheep chomping at the grass, it was easy to deceive yourself into believing that the owner of that beloved voice wasn't going to die. Laughter like that belonged to the strong, the hopeful, the living.

We naturally talked about other things besides cows and sheep. Royal wedding fever was in the air, Prince Charles was soon to marry Lady Diana, the entire country was in a state of suspense.

Ken, Evelyn and myself were on the island of Iona on the day of the wedding. It was bliss. We had the place to ourselves. Everyone was crowded into pubs, hotels, houses, anywhere and everywhere, glued to television sets.

Our world that day was Iona, the sun was at last shining. The Sound of Iona was a lake of pink and turquoise, wild flowers bloomed all over the machair, Ben More on Mull thrust its barren shoulders into an azure sky, the white doves of Iona were like ivory carvings on the ledges of the Abbey.

We breathed the sweet air of the holy isle and knew peace. I wished Mary could have been there, I wished so many things sitting there in Yellow Peril on the white sands of Martyr's Bay with Ken and Evelyn tranquil and thoughtful beside me. It was such a beautiful world, full of light and life and love.

We phoned Mary that night. Yes, she had had a wonderful day. She and her family had watched the wedding on TV. It had been a lovely wedding, she had enjoyed it so – and she had eaten half of a small steak pie without being sick – she was getting better.

Mary came back to her green hills in the September of that year. She was very near death. Her husband and family hadn't wanted her to come, it was a risk, she could die at any time and ought to be at home at the end.

We were willing to take that risk, Ken and Evelyn and I. I wanted her to see her bonny hills again, I wanted her to know a last holiday at Polly Powdermill, the dear little house she had loved right from the start.

She was very delicate, very thin. Mary, who had always been so comely and attractive and who had always wanted to be slim.

'I've got my wish at last, Chris,' she joked. 'I used to let all my clothes out, now Catherine takes them all in and still they're too big.'

She could barely eat anything. Ovaltine was about the one thing she lived on, that and pills, morphine amongst them. She slept a lot, in the car, on a chair. She would just fall asleep, in the middle of reading a book, during a conversation, and then she would awaken with a start, angry at herself but half-dazed with weariness.

The sun shone for her, it was warm and sheltered at the east door. I'll never forget Ken's kindness and consideration towards my darling sister. He padded a garden seat with pillows so that she could sit in comfort outside, her face to the sun, her eyes to the hills. Each night he filled a flask with Ovaltine and left it at her bed so that she wouldn't have to get up when she got thirsty. She had done that the first night and we had all been upset at the idea of so frail a being up and doing in a cold house, creeping about so that she wouldn't disturb the rest of us.

When she was sick he washed her clothes without question, waving aside her embarrassed protests that she could manage fine herself.

Oh Mary! Her heart pounding in her fragile breast, rising up in panic out of her chair, worried because someone else was doing the things she felt she should be doing herself with the last of her brave strength.

I would have anointed her with oil, kissed the tears from her face, taken her into my arms to tell her how much I loved her if any of these would have taken away her pain.

Because despite the morphia she suffered, pain was on her face, etched on her brow, it had superseded the laughter lines round her mouth.

Yet, despite all that the deception went on. Did she know? That was the question we kept asking ourselves, which we still ask ourselves to this day. Was she protecting us from the truth even while we were protecting her? If so, how lonely she must have been, how lonely and afraid and desperately needing comfort. For her sake I

171

longed so much for the pretence to stop.

We could have helped her face that last journey, we could have talked and told her how much she meant to us.

It was a terrible strain on us all, but only because of that. Otherwise it was a strangely peaceful time. Evelyn, who was sleeping in my caravan, would come up to the house each morning to have breakfast and go off to school. We took Mary for runs in the car, to Ardentinny, Loch Eck, Lock Fyne, all the places that she loved and wanted to see again. One day she managed to eat some ice cream and was so pleased with herself she sang a little song to herself on the way home, there in the car with lochs and hills speeding past and the autumn trees a blur of russet and gold.

Every other day Ken tucked her into my spare wheelchair and took her for walks with me alongside in Yellow Peril. The air smelt like apple and bramble wine; the rowan berries were like splashes of blood on the hill; the bracken was gold in the sun; red squirrels chattered in the trees and I was minded of last autumn when Mary had walked and laughed beside us, her face rosy and bright – but tired sometimes – I remembered that too and now I knew why.

She was very weak but even so she insisted on doing little things about the house, saying as she did so that she would never get any stronger if we kept on pampering her, and she would smile and look at me, and me never turning away from those honest, grey, questioning eyes.

She bought postcards to send to Australia. I can see her yet, sitting by the fire under the lamplight, her head down bent, her face in shadow, concentrating hard on what she was doing, fighting against the morphine, the pain and the sickness.

She showed me what she had written. Her pen had been

unsteady but the message on each card was clear enough. She told Kirsty and Margaret that she was having a lovely holiday with us, that she was sleeping well and eating like a horse and that she was golden brown from sitting all day in the sun.

To me those simple words were the final heartbreak. She knew she was dying, I'm convinced of that now, but then I couldn't be sure and the pretence had gone too far for it to stop.

Those carefully penned words to her sisters in Australia were an expression of her love for them. She wanted to spare them, to boost up their spirits and give them reason to hope. And it worked, over a divide of twelve thousand miles those brave words written by a dying woman made Kirsty and Margaret believe that Mary was on the mend and that those long, weary months of anxiety and dread were over with.

Perhaps it was a cruel reprieve. Who knows what is best at such a time? I only know that worry and sadness were lifted from their shoulders and that they knew peace for a little while.

A week went by and it was time for Mary to go home, but we urged her to stay longer and she seemed glad to accept. She brightened so much at the idea of a few more days at her beloved Polly Powdermill, she ate a good tea that evening and seemed much better altogether.

Two days later she came out of her room, looked at me and said, 'The time has come, Chris.'

Just that, nothing more, and the words so strange and final sounding that I forgot to be careful and just stared at her, the tears starting to my eyes. She comforted me then, that lovely smile coming swift to her mouth and a little

173

laugh as she said, 'Chris, Chris, it's all right, I just feel it's time I was with my family. I've had a lovely holiday but it's over.'

The next day we took her home. At the door she gazed at the hills for the last time. 'The summer's dying,' she spoke softly, almost to herself, 'yet whenever I think of your hills they are always green and alive, and so bonny.'

She slept most of the way home and it was a quiet journey. Ken and I never spoke except with our eyes, both of us heavy with pain and sorrow as the wheels sped the miles away.

Her husband was there to meet us and help her out of the car but she shook off his arm, defiantly, as if to let us all know that she was well enough to manage herself.

At the last moment she turned and looked at me, her eyes shining, shining, with some inner glow of strength, with sisterly love and warmth that reached out and encompassed the years we had shared together in trust and companionship.

'Chris.' she spoke suddenly, urgently. 'Never leave the cottage till you have done all there is to be done to it. It will be worth it in the end, I know it will. Take care of yourself, hen, take care of each other.'

She turned and walked away – and then she was at the window, both arms raised above her head, waving them back and forward – a final farewell? A last attempt to convince us that she was feeling on top of the world? A vision that we could carry with us for all time and remember a Mary who loved the green hills, and who had used up the last of her strength in order to spend the time that was left to her with people she loved in a place that she had loved from the first moment she had set eyes on it.

I never saw Mary again. A week or so later I went for a walk in my little Yellow Peril, Tania at my side, a look in her brown eyes that said, 'It's all right, Chris, I'm here, I'll always be here.'

It was October. The Wee Echaig was in spate. I sat and gazed at the tumbling brown waters and knew in my heart the bleakness and sadness of things yet to come.

And come they did. On the way back up that steep, hard brae, Ken's younger brother Scott, who stayed with Gran in the Holy Loch house, came along in his car. They had had a phone call. Mary, my beloved Mary was dead. Peacefully, they said. Well, they always said that. I hoped, prayed that it had been so.

Scott had the sense not to hang about. He knew what I was like. Perfectly composed I acknowledged the news and went on my way. It was a mild, tangy day, the air was filled with the sweetness of the heather, the rowans were red on the hill – and Mary wasn't here to share the beauty with me.

My treasured sister was dead, the autumn leaves were falling, whispering all around me as I went on up the hill to home, Tania plodding faithfully and silently by my side.

When later I learned that Mary hadn't been able to speak at the end, something inside me curled and died. To know that she had faced death without being able to voice a last fare-well was, for me, the final agony in a long year of waiting and wondering. Ken went alone to the funeral. I was too sick at heart to make that journey over the water to see my darling sister being laid to her last rest. In my heart the goodbyes had long ago been said and Ken understood. He knew how much Mary had always meant to me.

17

Pitfalls

The winter of 1981/82 brought some of the worst weather we had yet encountered in the glen. But it wasn't just country areas which suffered. Britain as a whole was experiencing dreadful weather conditions.

As the temperature plummeted several degrees below zero, diesel oil was freezing in fuel tanks, pipes were bursting all over the place and the plumbers of the nation became a much sought-after band of men.

As in previous winters we didn't have the worry of burst pipes to contend with, simply because we had no indoor tanks or a plumbing system in the cottage. But the water froze, of course. The water in the holding tank on the hill became one huge lump of solid ice; the burn was suspended in an icy grip; great fangs of ice hung from frozen waterfalls; even the very sea froze at its edges and the earth was rock hard.

Each morning we woke to thick sheets of ice inside the windows, a paraffin heater was kept burning all night in the sitting room and during the day Jockey was kept partially covered in an effort to keep him warm.

To go outside and draw breath in the viciously cold air

was a painful experience; the wild birds were dropping dead in alarming numbers. Some just froze to death in the night and it became quite a common occurrence to find their poor little bodies lying stiff under the trees. I almost cried when Evelyn found two dead robins under the sitting room window, those birds that remained alive were half-crazed with cold and hunger and it became a never-ending task putting out food for them and making sure that they had water to drink. They huddled on the window ledges, too miserable to even squabble with one another, one bold little blue tit took to chapping at our bedroom window with his beak in order to get us up out of bed and give him his breakfast.

I was never done making fat-cakes and filling up the nut containers; huge lumps of suet were nailed to the window surrounds so that the little creatures could feed without being blown away in the strong winds.

One morning we opened the east door and a wild dove walked in. Completely without fear, he toddled into the living room to stand in the middle of the floor and give a soft little 'coo, coo' of pleasure as the heat of the fire washed over him.

We were all entranced. It reminded me of a similar incident that had happened to me in my Govan days. One wintry night I was playing in the room with my brothers and sisters when there came a tap, tapping at the window. Engrossed in play, we at first ignored the sound, but it became so persistent one of us went to look. There on the ledge was a bedraggled grey pigeon, huddling against the window as if trying to escape the biting wind. Naturally we allowed him to come inside our domain and he was utterly delighted to snuggle into a shoe box lined with an old cardigan, there to partake of bread and bits of cheese and any other titbits we could smuggle in to him without Da getting wind of what we were up to.

For several days that pigeon stayed, allowing us to handle him and play with him and feed him, all with the utmost aplomb on his part.

When Da began to get suspicious we thought it was time Pink Eye went. With great regret we returned him to the ledge where he had first made his appearance, but could we get that bird to stay put long enough for the window to be closed on him? We jostled with him, we pushed him, we tried to make him fly off but he stuck to that ledge as if he was fixed to it with glue. In the end he won and back he came inside to spend one more night of pampered luxury.

Next day we took him in his shoe box to the nearby Elder Park and opened the lid a fraction so that we would be well away by the time he struggled out. That night we missed him badly. We mourned for him. But not for long! The very next morning he was at the *kitchen* window, chapping it for all he was worth, his head cocked, a most anticipatory expression in his bright eyes.

We were at the table at the time, gulping down our cocoa before going off to school. At sight of that bird we all looked at one another in dismay and I choked so much on my cocoa Mam thumped me soundly on the back.

As far as Da was concerned, I could have expired there and then and he wouldn't have noticed. He had eyes only for the window and Pink Eye, boldly chapping away and becoming quite indignant because his demands weren't gaining him immediate entry into the house.

'It's a pigeon,' Da spoke in wonderment, 'a bloody pigeon chappin' the window.'

The 'bloody pigeon' grew quite excited when Da went to the window and opened it. Before Da could stop him in he strutted, sure of a welcome, eyeing the table with interest. In his excitement at being back in the fold he squirted a moist dropping on to Mam's Monday-scrubbed lino and she was by no means amused.

'Get that dirty brute out o' here!' she ordered in no uncertain manner. We all looked at Da, wondering what his reaction would be, but I should have known. He was a bird lover, when he went to the park he often took a bag of crumbs to feed the wild birds and was always particularly pleased to feed the pigeons.

'Och, no, Evelyn,' he said somewhat sheepishly. 'It's pishin' wi' rain oot there. Chris,' he turned to me, 'go away ben the hoose and get that shoe box out o' the cupboard. The bird can stay in that till the rain goes off.'

Well, I went of course, knowing full well that the shoe box in question was lying under a bush somewhere in the Elder Park.

'It isn't there, Da,' I reported when I came back, having allowed a suitable time to elapse.

'Bloody weans, aye shifting things,' he grumbled. 'Never mind, we'll put it in that kindling box in the scullery, it'll be fine there for a wee while.' So saying he scooped up Pink Eye with one expert hand and deposited him into the hastily-emptied box that Margaret had rushed to bring from the scullery.

By the time we all got home from school Pink Eye had been returned to the wild, but every morning after that he came to the kitchen window to be fed and crooned to by Da who truly believed that he was the first and only one in the house to have been favoured by the pigeon's attentions.

When the spring came, Pink Eye's visits grew less and less and one day he went off never to return, much to Da's sorrow.

I had often thought about that pigeon and wondered why he had chosen to seek shelter in our house when there were so many others round about. Mam had said he had perhaps been a wandering soul who had taken on the guise of a pigeon, but whatever he was he had been a unique experience in my life.

Now here was a wild dove, standing in the middle of our living room, looking every inch what he was supposed to be with nothing ghostly or soul-like about him. Evelyn was thrilled to bits by the dove's presence. 'Let me keep it, let me keep it,' she begged. 'He can stay in my room, I'll get a cardboard carton from the shed and punch holes in it, he won't be any bother, I promise, I promise – and it will only be till the blizzards are past.'

She had quickly added that last condition on seeing the look on my face when the dove added his own particular contribution to the pattern on the hearthrug.

I had noticed too that in a very short space of time the dove's identity had leapt from 'it' to 'he' and now 'Coo-Coo' (Evelyn dreamed up the name within the first five minutes), and that he was lapping up the fuss and attention Evelyn was pouring over him.

The evidence was plain to see, my daughter had fallen in love with a rather sorry-looking bird, and if I didn't get that same bird out of the house within the next few minutes there would be no turning back.

Then I saw Evelyn's face, mutely appealing, and I suddenly remembered myself at her age, starry-eyed and daft about a bundle of grey feathers known as Pink Eye, and I

181

relented and went willingly to see what I could rustle up for Coo-Coo's breakfast.

So our strange and unexpected little visitor stayed cosy and safe in Evelyn's room and was quite content to remain there for the next three days. On the third morning he strutted to the east door and stood there looking up at us expectantly, much the same as Tania looked when she was tired of the house and wanted to get out of it for a while.

'I don't want him to go,' said Evelyn tremulously, 'he might never come back.'

'He belongs outside – the storm has passed and he knows it,' Ken said, as tactfully as he could.

'He might die out there, it's freezing cold,' Evelyn argued. But it was to no avail, Coo-Coo very definitely wanted his freedom and as soon as the door was opened he fluttered on to some nearby snowy branches, there to look at us for a few moments, before he was off, flying into the woods, and that was the last we saw of him.

We all wondered what had made him seek the shelter of our house. Perhaps he had been exhausted with cold and starvation and had known he would die if he didn't find rest and sustenance soon. Whatever had prompted him to come to us, his time with us had been a lovely experience, one that we would cherish.

Coo-Coo aside, we had our own survival to think about. The logs that had been stockpiled during the summer months diminished at an alarming rate, and even with the fires piled high the house remained cold and only grew cosy in the evenings when the curtains were tightly shut.

We read reports in the newspapers about toilet pans and cisterns shattering, as water turned to ice and expanded the vitreous enamel, so Ken made haste to drain ours before the same thing happened to us. Everyone in the village resorted to similar safety measures and the main topic of the day was the weather and the inconvenience it was causing in every household.

Christmas came and went in a very traditional atmosphere of frost and snow, and we bucked one another up by harping long and loudly on how nice it was to have a white Christmas.

January brought even more freezing conditions, together with snow storms that blocked the road, and made the whole business of living deep in a Highland glen a somewhat trying affair.

Ken and I were particularly depressed at this time. I hadn't gotten over the death of my darling Mary, and Ken was fretting because he felt we weren't much nearer improving the house than we had been when we had moved in more than three years ago.

Ken loved Polly Powdermill but, it has to be said, I cherished it more and could thole the inconveniences better than he. But then women do have much more resilience than men, and Ken would be the first to agree with me over that. The idea of looking for something else at that stage had never entered my head – but it had entered Ken's, and fate stepped in to take a hand, as it often does when the defences are down and you are looking for a way out of a situation that has become too much of a burden.

Our neighbour across the road spoke about a house that was for sale and going at a reasonable price. A cottage, he said, close to the sea with its own boathouse underneath and a nearby stone shed that would make an ideal study for me – and we would have our very own stretch of shore all to ourselves.

It sounded idyllic. Ken was all for rushing to see it and even I was caught up in the excitement of the moment – a boathouse – a study – our very own shore and jetty! Summer days; sunbathing; paddling; swimming; boating. The visions conjured themselves rapidly – one after another – and every one of these delights would be there on our own doorstep.

But what about our house, the lack of plumbing, the roof? The thousand and one things needing doing to it. We would never sell it the way it was.

Our neighbour reassured us on all points. He was in the property business. A deal could be struck, one house in exchange for another.

We could hardly wait for the roads to clear so that we could get to see this marvellous house in its perfect setting, and as soon as it was possible we all piled into our neighbour's car and off we went. Our goal lay on the other side of Dunoon – approximately seventeen miles the other side of it! Polly Powdermill, though deep in the country, was only three miles from the nearest shops; seven miles from Dunoon.

The road took us on and on into attractive country and then we were driving beside a long narrow inland sea loch. The hills rose up on either side, bonny hills, red with bracken, patched with evergreens, but in parts bare and dour – and somehow oppressive.

A brisk wind was churning up the loch, wisps of spray rose up like grey spectres out of the depths. I shivered and sensed something sad and eerie about this place, the brooding hills held secrets, the narrow loch looked dangerous and forbidding.

I had inherited this sense from Mam and had from time to

time in my life experienced strange and unexplained emotions about certain places that had stirred up apprehensions in some quiet, dark corner of my mind.

This loch, these hills, had that effect on me but it wasn't until later, when Ken explained some of the things that had happened there, that I knew why I had felt as I did whilst driving along the lonely shores.

During the war the Royal Navy commandos had trained there with the midget submarines, prior to attacking the German battleship, *Tirpitz*, which was lying low in a Norwegian fiord. Many of the landlocked Scottish lochs were similar to the fiords in Norway and so were suitable for a number of war-orientated practices. Many of the men who took part in the *Tirpitz* raid never returned and that might have been why I sensed their spiritual presence, roaming forever the quiet hills, the dour loch.

It is my belief that certain places retain atmospheres of tragedy. It is there in the field of Culloden where so many brave Scots were slain by the Duke of Cumberland's English army, and on the island of Mull there is a stretch of open moorland that is lost and lonely, even in daylight when the sun shines and the skylark sings. I wasn't surprised to learn of the Highland Clearances that had taken place on this part of the island, for I sensed the sadness, the desolation and despair, the very first time I came upon that moor, knowing nothing of these heartless evictions.

Today there is little to tell of that time, only one or two crofthouses dotted about, deserted, roofless, only the sough of the wind keening through empty windows, only the sheep huddling in grassy spaces that had once sheltered men, women, and children, laughing and talking by their peat fire blaze, never dreaming that one day they would be herded from their homes like cattle and forced to leave the land of their birth, forced to forsake their roots and their beloved glens and bens.

Sad, sad, is their Scotland now, eternally weeping for children gone from her shores, leaving behind a country that is lost and bewildered and poorly managed by people who have never understood her, nor ever will, for they have never known her earth and her hills and the strange strong beauty of blood and ties that never die, no matter the years and the distance that separate the exiles from their homeland.

The cottage was in the grounds of a fairly large estate, the road to it led off from the main driveway and petered out to a potholed track which was also full of ruts and bumps and was slippery with frozen mud.

It stood in a hollow and the road was almost level with the eaves. The access was terrible. There was no garden, a dank, rough slope led to a narrow door, and there was a step up into the house. This turned out to be half the size of Polly Powdermill and was soon explored.

A large kitchen was dismally illuminated by two narrow windows that looked seawards. Two other rooms had bigger windows but were so small they wouldn't have made decent bedrooms and neither were suitable as living rooms. The poky bathroom was cramped and miserable and made our cludge seem opulent in comparison.

Opposite the house was a steep, overgrown incline and somewhere in its wooded depths was the water supply. In that jungle of undergrowth it was probably more liable to silting and freezing than our own supply in the glen. But the roof of the house looked decent enough and there was no evidence of leaks in any of the rooms. The water was also plumbed in and there was an immersion heater in the tank.

'There wouldn't be enough rooms,' I commented as we all stood in the kitchen, 'it would be like jumping from the frying pan into the fire.'

I could have said more but not with our neighbour there. His intentions might have been good but it was obvious he didn't understand our requirements as a literary and artistic family.

Despite the inadequacies of the house I could see Ken's mind ticking over, and the next minute he voiced his thoughts, saying that access could be made from inside the house to the boathouse below, which would make a fine big living room with a picture window looking out to sea.

I didn't bother to point out that it would be beyond me to descend to such a room, I simply was not taking the affair seriously – but Evelyn was.

'I could sleep in a caravan,' she clamoured excitedly. 'In fact I could *live* in it and cook my own food and have my own TV.'

Eleven years old and already she wanted to set up home! Her face was red, her voice high with excitement. I saw no point in even mentioning that there was no TV reception in this hill-enclosed part of the country, since I could see plainly enough that both she and Ken were throwing practicalities to the wind in their eagerness to try and make this small, cramped cottage a feasible proposition.

It would of course be a summer idyll, that I had to admit. It was mild that day, the snow was fast melting from the hills, those brooding hills across the loch. But the sun came out, gilding the bracken to gold, taking away the dourness, laving the dark loch with spangles of light that shimmered and danced – and it was all there, right on the doorstep.

And the boathouse beneath the cottage was a fine, big, airy place, and it contained a motor boat that was in with the price. A sturdy stone shed near the house could be lined and decorated and turned into a lovely little study – and its window faced towards the sea, a sea no longer black and forbidding but blue and beautiful in the sunlight.

I too was then caught up on the tide of enthusiasm and when Ken grabbed my chair and pushed me on to the jetty and drew a word picture of what it would be like for me to sit there writing my books, I forgot all my earlier doubts and just gazed and gazed at the hills and the loch. Then I saw a large shed a little distance from the house with a long, gradual slipway leading into the water. On enquiring what the shed was for, our neighbour told us it had been used to house the midget submarines during the war.

The information meant nothing to me at the time, but even so a shiver went through me and at that moment the sun slid behind a cloud and the hills were dark once more.

And quite unbidden Mary's voice spoke in my mind and I heard the last words she had ever said to me, 'Never leave Polly Powdermill till you have done all there is to be done to it...Never leave...Never leave...'

We visited the cottage three times after that and each time something always seemed to happen to Marilla Mini. The first time she got stuck on the icy incline leading from the driveway; the second time she got bogged down in a muddy pothole and, as there was no one around to help, Ken laboured for ages to get her out again; the third time she got well and truly jammed in a hard-packed snowy rut and had to be towed out by another car which fortunately came by after we had sat half-frozen for almost an hour.

And then one night Mary came to me in a dream, only it was so real I felt as if she had somehow plucked me out of my own body and was carrying me swiftly and effortlessly through aeons of time and space that were beyond my understanding.

Yet I felt no fear, Mary was beside me, guiding me, keeping me safe. No words were spoken, yet we communicated, and suddenly we were inside the house by the sea and one by one she led me to each window. I knew that I was at a great height for when I looked I saw that the walls plunged downwards, straight into the depths of the dark, deep sea. My stomach churned with fear and I didn't want to see more, but then I was at the next window and the next, Mary at my side, silent and supportive but making me look, making me face the black, horrifying depths far below.

'Pitfalls.' She spoke that one word, nothing more, and then I was back in my bed, waking, remembering every detail of that strange, terrifying dream. I lay for a long time, thinking about it, remembering the horror, and I felt safe, so safe in my own bed, in my own bedroom, Polly Powder-mill serene and silent all around me.

When I told Ken about my dream he looked at me for a long time. He didn't laugh or tell me that my imagination was working overtime, instead he was serious and quiet and very sincere when he eventually spoke.

'She was warning us, Chris, not to make a move. She's still here with us, advising us, helping us. She loved this house, she had faith in it, the other house would never have worked for us, she knew it and she warned us.'

189

And that was that. Outside the window the birds were singing, the sun had come back to the mill, the snowdrops were blooming, the daffodils peeping, the worst winter we had ever known was over and done with, spring would soon be here with its drowsings and its dreamings, its blue skies and its green hills.

The urge for change had left Ken as swiftly as it had come. Evelyn had already forgotten the other house, she had only seen it once, she was too busy watching the ditches for frog spawn to bother her head about anything else. For me it had all been more of an adventure than anything else, but a dangerous adventure for all that. I had been tempted, I had allowed myself to be swept along by the tide because it was easier to give in than to resist.

Mary had known that, she had pulled me back. Since her death she had never come to disturb my dreams and that was why I knew that that one dream was so important, the message in it had to be obeyed.

My memories of her are as strong and as loving as ever, but to this day she has never again come to me in a dream.

She was too gentle and peaceful in life to ever want to haunt anyone in death, but just the same, I know she's there. Like Mam, she's always there, watching over me and mine, a guiding light that never dims.